R.B Saville Peck

H.R.H. PRINCESS MARINA
DUCHESS OF KENT

H.R.H.
PRINCESS MARINA
Duchess of Kent

The First Authentic Life Story

by

J. WENTWORTH DAY

LONDON
ROBERT HALE LIMITED
63 Old Brompton Road, S.W.7

PRINTED IN GREAT BRITAIN
BY EBENEZER BAYLIS AND SON, LTD.
THE TRINITY PRESS, WORCESTER, AND LONDON

Contents

Illustrations

ILLUSTRATIONS

between pages 104 *and* 105

Philip de Laszlo's portrait of Princess Nicholas provides a background to this photograph of her daughter

The Duchess with her son, the second Duke of Kent, photographed on the eve of their departure for the Far East in 1952

facing page

CHAPTER ONE

The Gipsy's Prophecy

TWO SMALL GIRLS, one gipsy-dark, the other blue-eyed, fair-haired, with a June-rose skin, sat rigidly on a sofa, holding hands. The room, book-lined, was dominated by a great desk. The notepaper upon it bore Royal arms. The two little girls had been told to keep quiet and be good for Mummy was very ill.

Outside, sunlight spilled pale champagne on white garden walls. A surge of bougainvilleas and oleanders rimmed a green sea of lawn. Blue sky and sailing white clouds above. A blue sea glittering to a horizon of purple islands far beyond the white girdle of garden walls. A day of sun and gaiety.

Yet the great white house was silent as death. The tall Doric pillars which framed the entrance, the high windows, classic lines, and stone balustrade on the flat roof gave it a Nash-like quality. But for the fact that this was a December day the house might well have been one of those square, white Georgian mansions which give grace to Regent's Park. But you do not see bougainvilleas in full bloom on a London day in December.

Upstairs, in a darkened room with the sun-blinds down, a woman with raven hair and a classic face lay silent in bed. Doctors and nurses, white-clad, moved quietly. It was the moment between life and death—and two Royal lives were at stake.

In the house, and in gilt-domed churches in the city without, men and women prayed silently.

Suddenly, in that dim room of filtered sunlight, a tiny cry, much as a kitten might make, broke the whispering stillness. A doctor left the room. A courtier, waiting below, heard the news.

Minutes later, in the city where houses and churches sprawled like scattered jewels between mountains and the sea, silver bells rang out from high and gilded steeples. Cannon boomed, dully, from mountain fortresses. Guns flashed from men-o'-war riding out at sea. The thunder of them rolled far off on the horizon among the Isles of

Greece. On all those isles of asphodel and olives, from Samothrace to the pillared ruins of Rhodes, the news rang.

Athens, classic cradle of civilization, saluted a babe in her cradle.

Daughter of a Royal prince, grand-daughter of a King and a Kaiser, great-niece of the Tsar of All the Russias, descended on her father's side from the Royal House of Glucksburg, monarchs of Denmark, on the other side from the Romanoffs, the fabulous dynasty of Russia, the tiny thing in her mother's arms opened her eyes upon a world of splendour and power immutable. Or so it seemed, in that age of thrones and empires, on December 13th, 1906.

Very lovely and quite unusual eyes. For they were golden-brown, the colour of amber, rimmed with green, large and mischievous.

When her grandparents, King George I of Greece and Queen Olga, walked upstairs and entered the big room, full of dusky sunlight, the tall King, with sweeping cavalry moustaches, looked down on the tiny thing whence had come the kitten cry and said, tenderly: "I suggest you call her Marina. She was one of the best loved of all the Greek saints, you know."

When one of her godmothers, the Princess of Wales, heard that hauntingly uncommon name, she wrote: "I think it is the prettiest name I have ever heard."

Little did she know that the tiny child with the enchanting eyes would one day become her own daughter-in-law.

For long after her daughter's birth, Princess Nicholas was desperately ill. A fragile wreck. Prince Nicholas, desperately anxious, took her for a course of treatment at Franzenbad two years running. During that time they paid a visit to our own King Edward VII who was at Marienbad. The centre of all eyes, the target of many ladies.

Prince Nicholas has many tales of their tricks to attract Royal notice. One American lady called "Caesar", King Edward's rough-haired terrier, to her. She grabbed him by the collar, took a pair of scissors out of her bag and snipped a tuft of hair from the indignant "Caesar's" tail.

"There," she said, triumphantly. "If I haven't anything else belonging to the King of England, at least I've part of his dawg."

She had the hair mounted in a locket and, says, Prince Nicholas, "Wore it always, exhibiting it with as much pride as though it had been part of the King's own hair".

There is a tale, I believe true, that some months after Princess Marina's birth, a gipsy-woman, old and wrinkled, came down from the grey-green olive groves on a mountain-side that had seen the purple-sailed navies of Tyre and Sidon glide by long centuries before. The old woman, looking like a sibyl from the mystic Grecian past said, flatly: "She is a child of destiny, and there is both sunshine and shadow for her. She will be beautiful and make a great marriage with a king's son. Love will be her guiding star. It will bring her sorrow, for she will lose her husband while she is still young and at the height of her happiness. But she will find consolation in her children."

That fantastic prophecy was fulfilled in all too-terrible truth. Within a few years thrones and empires born of the splendour and power of centuries, crashed. Europe ran with blood. The city of Athens was shelled and bombarded by French and English guns. The child's grandfather, who chose for her that haunting name, was shot dead by a madman. Her own family were hounded out of home and country, hunted from pillar to post by the ebb and flow of the greatest war that ever shook the world.

In those first, few, formative years the child who was to grow to breathtaking, classic loveliness, the most elegant princess of her time and age, saw the last splendours of the Russian Court in all its almost barbaric magnificence. She saw too, as a child, those who had been noble, gallant and great, near starvation in the back-streets of Paris.

When peace came and the thrones of Greece and Yugoslavia were shakily rebuilt, she, who the gipsy had said would marry a great king's son for love alone, was courted in the modern way, by a Royal suitor who flew, high over the mountains and fir-forests of the turbulent Balkans, to ask her for her hand in a fairy-tale villa on the edge of a lake ringed by mountains and forests.

Then the wedding in the dim splendour of Westminster Abbey, before the gilded reredos of the altar, in a flicker of tall candles, a blaze of uniforms. And outside the roar of the London crowds, the homely warmth of an English welcome to its loveliest princess.

In the abyss of time the gipsy prophecy loomed, to those who remembered it, with grim foreboding. It came true. In the agony and bloody suffering of that Second World War which put out the lights of Christ and civilization over half Europe. A flying-boat, roaring north through the Scottish mists, crashed into a desolate hillside. The husband she adored, the father whose youngest son had been christened only a week or so before, was killed. The old sibyl from the olive groves, inspired by Heaven knows what mystic instinct, had prophesied with ghastly truth.

There is a little of the light and shade in the life of Her Royal Highness, Princess Marina, Duchess of Kent, the most tragic member of the
Royal family. Today, as the Greek hag foretold, she has found her
supreme and lasting consolation—her children. And in her invincible
sense of Royal duty.

Many people instinctively think of Princess Marina as the glass
of fashion, the mould of elegance—the chic leader of quiet good taste
—a life clouded by one tragedy only.

The truth is that her life, almost from the earliest years, was rocked
by violent contrasts of tragedy and happiness.

She came, in the first place, from a Royal house which, in less than
a hundred years, has known more deaths and upheavals than probably
any other Royal house in Europe. Consider the trail of tragedy.

Classic Greece died when Alexander fell dead on the battlefield with
Pyrrhus two thousand years ago. Modern Greece was re-born just
over a century ago. Byron was its champion, its troubadour, its
Roland of the Singing Sword, against the "tyrannous Turk". The
British Admiral Codrington led the Allied Fleet which smashed the
Turks at Navarino in 1827 and gave Greece independence.

A year later she became a republic under Capodistria. He was
assassinated. Thus the first of the modern rulers of Greece knew the
taste of murder and tragedy. More were to follow that grim path.

Greece decided to become a kingdom. The throne was offered to
Leopold of Saxe-Coburg-Gotha, the Royal house which gave us
Albert, the Prince Consort. Leopold refused the Crown.

Otto of Wittlesbach, Prince of Bavaria, accepted it. With true
Bavarian thoroughness he gave Greece thirty years of hell and tyranny.
Then they kicked him out. He was expelled.

In 1863 the throne of Greece was offered to H.R.H. The Duke of
Edinburgh. Greece wanted an English king. The Duke refused it.
So they asked the Earl of Derby to be King. He also refused. Lan-
cashire was safer.

Prince William of Schleswig-Holstein, the Danish Duchy soon to
be seized by Prussia, accepted the crown. He reigned as King George I
of Greece. His wife, Queen Olga, daughter of the Grand Duke Constantine of Russia, is still spoken of lovingly in Greece today as "Queen
Olga the Good". One of King George's sisters was our own beloved
Queen Alexandra, whose Rose Day yearly commemorates her name
and memory. Another sister was Tsarina of Russia.

King George I had five sons. The eldest, Constantine, married

Princess Sophia, sister of Kaiser Wilhelm II of Germany. The third son, Prince Nicholas, married the Grand Duchess Helen of Russia in 1902 and to them were born three daughters, Olga, now Princess Paul of Yugoslavia; Elizabeth, Countess Toerring-Yettenbach, who died a few years ago; and Princess Marina, Duchess of Kent.

George I, as I have said, was shot by a madman in 1913. That was the price he paid for being a democratic king. He always walked among his people unarmed. The humblest man could speak to him. He visited their homes. He never worked less than ten hours a day. He had tact, sincerity, an open heart, a clear head and a fair mind.

He accepted the Crown when he was only eighteen years of age, a naval cadet with his heart set on a career in the Danish Navy. He did so only because his father and his great-uncle, King Frederick VII of Denmark, told him that it was his duty to do so.

Four years later his Greek counsellors told him that he should go to Russia and marry a Grand Duchess. They already had one in view. He chose a different one.

One day he called on the Grand Duke Constantine. A dark-eyed, dark-haired, fifteen-year-old girl, with classic features and impish eyes looked down at him over the balusters of the great marble staircase as he stood in the gilded splendour of the hall in the Grand Ducal Palace.

A few months later he married her. She set sail for Greece with a huge trunkful of dolls and toys. Such was the Duchess of Kent's grandmother—a marriage, like her own, not of State design but for love at first sight.

Their third son, Prince Nicholas, later to be Marina's father, loved painting, poetry, books, the theatre, and beauty in all its guises. He had a rare sense of humour, a devout sense of duty, a firm faith in God. These qualities have descended to his daughter.

We will come to the assassination of King George I later. Consider, for the moment, the pattern of tragedy which followed. His son, Constantine, nicknamed King Tino, succeeded. That was on the threshold of the First World War in 1914. War broke out between England, France, Russia, their Allies, and Germany. King Constantine was torn between pressure from the Kaiser, his wife's brother—whom incidentally, she disliked—and pressure from England and Russia. His own instinct was to keep Greece neutral. He had already won a war against Turkey and he knew that his army and the country could not afford to fight another war. He put his duty to Greece before the powerful wire-pullings of Venizelos, his coldly opportunist Prime Minister, and Lloyd George.

The Allies demanded his abdication. Abused, misrepresented, his summer palace set on fire about his ears, his Queen almost burnt alive, he left the throne on June 12th, 1917, saying, "I am going away for the time being." Princess Marina was then eleven—old enough to realize the humiliation and tragedy of it all.

With the king went his heir, George, Duke of Sparta. He had served in the Prussian Guards when no one thought that Germany would go to war. For that he was barred from the Crown. Greece crowned his brother as King Alexander—the first of that name since Alexander the Great. Three years later he was bitten by a pet monkey, poisoned, died. He left a daughter, Queen Alexandra of Yugoslavia.

Greece recalled Constantine. He came back to find that Venizelos had left him with a legacy of war. Turkey, the old enemy, hammered at the gates, thirsting to re-conquer the lands that had groaned beneath the taxes and tortures of her Sultans. King Constantine, no coward, led an ill-disciplined, ill-armed army against the old enemy. At first he won resounding victories. Then a bitter winter of snow and privation followed. It sapped the strength and courage of the Greek Army.

When the summer came, King Constantine's army, bogged down, far from its base, was attacked by the Turkish guns and cavalry, their planes and infantry. Mustapha Kemal, the maker of modern Turkey, a born soldier, had re-formed and re-organized his own army during the winter. The Greek Army, obedient to the dictates of the Allies, England and France, had sat tight waiting for help which never came. The result was that the Turks went through the Greek Army like knives through butter. King Constantine's men were shattered, scattered, slaughtered and taken prisoner. The Turks sacked the city of Smyrna in a welter of blood and torture unequalled since the Middle Ages.

And King Constantine, the innocent victim of Power politics, intrigued against by Venizelos, let down by Lloyd George and by France, was branded as the scapegoat. He was deposed, hounded out of the country—and died three months later of a broken heart.

Thus tragedy, frustration, death and defeat dogged the Greek Royal family like the Ravens of Odin.

King Constantine's son, Prince George, succeeded his father as King George II of the Hellenes in 1922. A mere puppet King, virtually a prisoner in his own palace. Venizelos, the Prime Minister, a coldly calculating opportunist, part Turk, part Jew, part Armenian, ruled as dictator. The Treasury was almost bankrupt.

Five loyal Greek Cabinet Ministers and the Commander-in-Chief of the Army, were clapped in prison and then hustled out one grey morning, without trial, without time to say their prayers, put against a wall and shot like dogs. Europe was appalled.

Prince Andrew of Greece, the present Duke of Edinburgh's father, was also in gaol, due to be shot. His fair-haired son little knew that his father's life hung in the balance by a matter of hours.

A personal friend of my own, Mr. Gerald Talbot, later knighted for his services, flew at breakneck speed from London to Athens with a personal letter from King George V of England, protesting strongly against the proposed murder of Prince Andrew. The Prince's life was saved at the eleventh hour.

That breakneck dash by Talbot may even have saved the life of the child who was to become Duke of Edinburgh—for Venizelos was in the mood for Royal murder. Russia had set the pattern with the utterly barbaric murder of the Tsar and his family.

The wretched King George II was deposed. All members of the Greek Royal family were forbidden ever to set foot on Greek soil again. Their houses and estates were confiscated.

Luckily, Prince Christopher of Greece, Princess Marina's uncle, managed to smuggle a little of her father's fortune, her mother's jewels and his own bonds and securities out of Greece in a rowing boat. He was nearly betrayed by her mother's pet cat!

For the second time Princess Marina, then sixteen years old, was sent into exile with her parents and two sisters—hounded out of the country to take refuge in Paris and fight the world on a shoe-string income. The exploits of the Scarlet Pimpernel are tame reading by comparison with the tragic adventures of the Duchess of Kent's own family.

That is the bare skeleton, the merest outline of the wars, murders, abdications and expulsions, the riches and poverty, the clashes of loyalties which clouded, like April storms, the childhood and the youth of the girl who was to capture the heart of Britain.

CHAPTER TWO

Childhood

THE FIRST seven years of Princess Marina's childhood were, mercifully, free of tragedy and sudden death. That may sound strange to British ears. Here, where law and order are the rule and not the exception, the thought of a Royal assassination is fantastic.

Yet in pre-1914 days, the bomb, the dagger and the bullet were the haunting fear behind every throne in Latin, Slav and Balkan countries.

Anarchists, Nihilists, and, later, Bolsheviks and the rest of the ghastly crew of "liberators of the people" flourished in underground cellars, back-street cafés, dockside bawdy houses and bandits' mountain hideouts. They were the architects of death. Today, their Communist successors are the apostles of world misery. The high priests of Antichrist. They, and their like, sent the Tsar of Russia and his family to a ghastly death in a blood-sprayed cellar at Ekaterinberg. Since then the clanking cattle-trucks rumbling across Russia carting tens of thousands to a living death in the salt-mines; the mass-murders in the Polish forests; the blood-bath in Hungary—all these are the logical outcome, the death-spawn of anarchy. We pay the price today in a world armed—according to the doctrine of Lenin—for final suicide with the H-bomb.

These horrors were far from the white-walled gardens of the great white house in the shining city of Athens. The house that was the little Princess Marina's childhood home. It was given to her mother, Princess Nicholas, by the Tsar as a wedding present. It looks more like an English country house of Georgian grace than a Royal palace. It is neither huge nor pretentious. But it had English bathrooms, hot and cold running water, heated towel rails. These were rare and enviable amenities in 1907. Even the Royal palace, vast and ugly, had no such comforts. The King himself only had one bathroom in the whole of his palace—and the taps seldom ran.

The little Princess's family life was governed by her father's strict sense of duty and discipline; his love of art; and his sense of humour.

Family group: Princess Marina (seated in front) with her mother and two
sisters, Princess Olga (left) and Princess Elizabeth

Princess Marina's father and his parents: King George I of Greece and Queen Olga and their third son, Prince Nicholas

Her mother, daughter of the Grand Duke Vladimir Alexandrovitch of Russia, brother of Tsar Nicholas II, and his wife, the Grand Duchess Maria Pavlovna, was deeply religious, devoted to her children, with a sense of mysticism inherent in her Russian blood. She, like Queen Olga of Greece, had a deep and sincere religious faith. It never deserted them, even when poverty, humiliation and physical suffering almost overwhelmed the Queen in later years.

Luckily for Princess Marina there was no strict code of Royal etiquette such as that which governed the Imperial Courts of Russia and Germany.

King George of Greece, her grandfather, held the most democratic Court in Europe. He loathed formality and unnecessary pomp. He walked about the streets, completely unaffected, ready and willing to talk to anyone. Often he would enter the humblest Greek home, listen to their troubles and put them straight. No king in Eastern Europe was more adored.

Prince Nicholas held the same views as his father. He brought up his three girls on the same lines. They led a healthy, unaffected life, romping in the garden with their grey mongrel puppy and a troop of tame rabbits. The servants were not allowed to address them as "Your Royal Highness" until each child was old enough to understand and carry with dignity her Royal responsibilities.

The result was that although Princess Marina, perhaps more than any of them, was strong-willed, determined and unquenchable, she was never bumptious. Her two sisters, Princess Olga and Princess Elizabeth, discovered by the time she was three or four years old, that although they could mother her they could never boss her. Baroness Helena von der Hoven, who knew the Greek Royal family well, says: "Her nurses and parents found out, too, that the little newcomer, who gurgled so happily in her cot, could be induced by kindness to do anything but would not be driven."

She loved dolls. Particularly Mary. Mary was a very special doll. She was taken for walks round the garden. Then she was undressed and put to bed. In the morning she was wakened, dressed carefully, with the right number of clothes and the right sort of clothes. Then her tiny "mother" made her bed the right way, tucking in the sheets and blankets and turning them down perfectly.

When Princess Marina was asked why Mary was such a favourite she answered simply: "I like her very much. I like her face."

Mary, indeed, became a sort of Crown Princess to the young

Princess. For when the three children went out for a drive in an open Victoria or landau drawn by high-stepping carriage horses with proud necks and jingling harness, a coachman, cockaded, breeched and booted, stately on the box, and a nanny sitting primly beside them, the warm-hearted Greek crowds went mad with joy and cheerful devotion. They adored their man-in-the-street King. They worshipped his three little grandchildren. So the children, naturally, were taught to bow right and left to the cheering crowds and to wave back to them.

Princess Marina occasionally became a little bored. Being a Great Lady, when you were really quite a little one, had its drawbacks. So she made Mary deputize for her.

"It hurts my neck to bow, and Mary will do the bowing now," she announced. So Mary was held up in one tiny hand whilst the other hand inclined Mary's neck and waved Mary's hand to the crowds. It was the supreme winner.

Her sister, Princess Elizabeth, also had a family of dolls. Oddly enough, they were all little girl dolls. So Princess Elizabeth knelt one night by her small bed and prayed for a little boy. She was bitterly disappointed when, after a week of supplication, God failed to give her a "son".

She complained about it to Princess Marina. The latter, always utterly logical, said sagely: "God probably has not had any time yet to make even *half* a little boy. Just wait—and keep on praying."

She was right. A week later, a wise and understanding grown-up presented little Princess Elizabeth with a boy doll. All was well. The power of prayer had been vindicated.

Whenever the family went away Princess Marina always packed her dolls' clothes most carefully in a box. The box was then put in her own trunk. Later in life she became a most careful and efficient packer-up, and, indeed, today, I am told she prides herself that she can pack more things into one box than anyone else—without creasing them.

Her love of children, which began with Mary and the other dolls, soon crystallized into complete adoration of other babies. The tinier and more helpless they were, the longer she would stand and peer into the cradle with utter devotion. If she was playing on the lawns and a perambulator passed the palace gates she would drop the game immediately and run at top speed for a peep at the baby, no matter whose it might be.

Her kingly grandfather could walk the streets of Athens and chat with passers-by but even his democracy was completely outclassed by that of his small grandchild. She sat down in the middle of the tram-lines! Her English governess picked her up and said firmly that if she did it again she would be spanked. Princess Marina promptly sat down again, slap in the middle of the lines.

Spankings in the Royal family had a faintly literary flavour. Princess Marina explained it to a friend, who asked her what paper she got as a child.

"*The Times*," replied the Princess, with that whimsical smile which is so much of her charm.

"Surely you didn't read *The Times* when you were a small child," the friend exclaimed.

"No, but I was spanked with it! So I am familiar with it since my earliest days."

Prince Nicholas told the inside story of this early acquaintanceship with journalism to Baroness von der Hoven. He was sitting reading *The Times* one day when little Princess Olga, the elder sister, flew into a tantrum. Her governess, in despair, asked Prince Nicholas to deal with his daughter. He promptly rolled up *The Times* and, stifling a smile, spanked her with it. Thereafter it became the rod of authority.

The greatest single influence in Princess Marina's young life, apart from that of her own family, was her English governess, Miss Fox.

"Foxy" ranks high in the immortal pageant of English governesses who, for a hundred and fifty years, with their pince-nez, reticules and high-necked blouses, have ruled the offspring of the great to the four corners of the earth. She joined the Greek Royal family when the three children were tiny mites. She remained a firm family friend, a wise adviser and a tower of strength to the three Princesses until the day of her death a few years ago.

True, they were given French and German governesses to instruct them in the language and manners of those countries but "Foxy", complete with gold pince-nez, was the calm court of final appeal, the ultimate mentor. Even political crisis, when it came ultimately, be-tween Britain and Greece, did not part them for long. Later when Princess Marina became Duchess of Kent and her own children were born, she insisted that "Foxy" should be there. To "Foxy" she turned in her own bitter grief when her husband was killed. The wise heart and the loving hand that had cared for her in childhood were her comfort in that final tragedy.

Princess Marina learnt from her English fairy-tales and English nursery-rhymes, just as she learnt from her father the immortal tales of Hans Andersen. Every Sunday afternoon the three little girls clustered around Miss Fox under the shade of a tree in the garden while she told them Bible stories for an hour before tea.

They learnt their first prayers in English, although they were all members of the Greek Orthodox Church, and kept each one of its Festivals. Princess Marina insisted on saying her good night prayers in English and not in Greek. When her grandmother, Queen Olga, asked her why she would not pray in Greek, she replied, with simple finality: "I've arranged it with God. I told Him I liked to talk to Him in English best, and he said: 'Please yourself, Marina. All languages are the same to me.'"

Another enchanting story concerns the evening when she was told to go to bed at six o'clock and say her prayers like any other good little girl. She meant to stay up.

"Lots of other little girls are going to bed now," she argued. "God must be terribly busy listening to all their prayers. If I go to bed later on, the rush will be over and God will have more time to listen to me."

God was, and still is, a very real Being in her life. When her father lectured her for some infant misdoing and told her that she ought to tell God she was sorry for being naughty, she looked him straight in the eye and said:

"What would be the use? If God knows everything He must know I'm sorry without being told. I don't want to waste His time."

This devastating logic of hers, usually uttered with a mischievous smile, was invincible. It defeated everyone. For example, she did not like music lessons. So her father sat down at the piano and started picking out nursery-rhymes on the keys with one finger. She watched him solemnly.

"Come along," he said, "you see Papa trying, don't you?"

"Yes," she answered, with that quick, mischief-lit smile, "that's why I don't."

Papa retired, defeated.

Mademoiselle Perrin, her French governess, gives an endearing little picture of her at the age of six . . . "Rather small for her age but she had a lovely face, the striking feature of which was a pair of vivacious eyes which seemed to light up her little face.

"I remember how delighted she was when I had a headache. She could come to my room pretending to be the doctor and put cold compresses on my forehead. In doing so she saturated my bedclothes!

"It was a relief to me when her nurse took her to the Royal Gardens where she would play with her cousins until lunchtime.

"All the family met at lunch, a meal we enjoyed very much. Princess Olga and Princess Elizabeth used to ask all sorts of questions. Princess Marina did not ask questions. She *answered* them, sometimes very cleverly."

Mademoiselle Perrin remembered that even at that early age Princess Marina would stand and stare at her father's paintings and drawings and try to copy them.

Prince Nicholas was a painter of outstanding merit. He learnt drawing as a boy under Monsieur Gillieron, a delightful old Swiss who was not only a first-rate artist but an erudite archaeologist. His notable work included a series of water-colours of the superb Byzantine frescoes of the churches of Mistra near Sparta, for the Marquess of Bute. He also copied the head and figure of the Virgin Mary and the saints on the inside western wall of the Acropolis. These unique murals dated from the time when the ancient classic temple was converted to a Christian church. Today they have faded almost to nothingness.

Prince Nicholas not only learnt drawing from this clever and charming old Swiss, but, with his father, King George I, who was a very knowledgeable archaeologist, he followed every step of the excavations at the Acropolis and saw Ancient Grecian temples brought to light which had been built long before the Parthenon.

It was in this atmosphere of keen artistic sense and delight in beauty that Princess Marina learned her first childish love of painting. Her father taught her and encouraged her. Today she is an accomplished artist in her own right, a skilled draughtswoman, a good painter in oils and pastels. She began to draw, as tiny children do, at the age of three or four—shaky lines, odd shapes, spirals, circles, curves and the rest. Soon the wiggles and squiggles took shape. The small girl produced a recognizable drawing of the Acropolis itself. This delighted her father. He took her in hand seriously. Before long she could not only draw, but paint. She began by colouring frocks on the figures in magazines. Then she cut out "little people" from a sheet of paper and painted their clothes and faces.

When she was not painting or mothering her dolls she was running a grocer's shop at which her sisters could do their shopping, or holding a "little people's tea party".

Apart from her dolls her favourite toys were minute china dishes, cups, plates and saucers, none of them much more than an inch long. She had a stock of tiny, imitation joints of meat, vegetables, fish, loaves of bread, sausages, carrots, cucumbers, cabbages, puddings and pats of butter, of microscopic size. They were all set out with the utmost care and attention to detail, either for a dinner party, a tea-party or on minute market stalls when she "went into trade".

Later on she was given a stove with a miniature oven and a set of saucepans. She baked biscuits, cooked dishes and became quite a knowledgeable cook by the time she was ten or eleven.

The little princesses were dressed usually in blue, pink or white, with matching bows in their hair. It was the fashion to have billows of white muslin for parties with lots of lace insertions and fanciful tucks. White, laced-up kid boots were occasionally worn whilst most little girls wore charming white knickers, lace-edged with small, white petticoats. All undergarments were white. Hats varied from sun-bonnets to floppy hats, tied under the chin with a large white muslin bow. I have seen one photograph of Princess Marina in her pram wearing the most fetching white, fluffy bonnet which flared out over the ears, with the brim coming to a vee over her nose. She knew how to wear a hat to the utmost advantage, even in those days. Like all younger sisters her main ambition was to keep up with her elder sisters. She was determined not to be left behind.

Yet she adored her sisters, and if anyone told her that she was a pretty little girl, she immediately answered:

"Wait until you see my sisters. They're lovely."

Then, if her sisters' good looks were admired, she went one better.

"Yes, they're lovely, but have you seen my mother? She's still more beautiful."

Which reminds one of a story told by Prince Nicholas. His mother, Queen Olga of Greece, was attending a State dinner. She put on her jewels. Thus, glittering, regal, imposing, she went to say good night to her two daughters. One little girl stared, and burst out with:

"You look like the Fairy Queen."

"She doesn't," her little sister said instantly, "she looks like God's wife."

Prince Nicholas brought up his three daughters, if not exactly in the "hard" way, at any rate with a strong emphasis on discipline, exercise, simplicity and good manners.

His own régime as a boy had been utterly Spartan. In his own words:

"We got up at six o'clock in the morning, winter and summer, were driven into a cold bath and had to be at our desks by 6.30. Doctor Luders [their tutor] arrived for breakfast at 7. Then lessons from 7.30 to 9.30, the hour for a second breakfast with our parents . . . This meal was despatched in half an hour and then were more lessons from ten to twelve. After that, one hour was devoted to fencing and the other to a wild romp in the Royal gardens. . . . At one o'clock we were well scrubbed and went up to our mother's rooms for lunch. Classes were resumed from two to four, followed by riding, gymnastics or an improving walk with our tutor. Preparations from five to seven under the sharp eye of Doctor Luders. . . . Then we dressed for dinner—this time in my father's room—and were in bed by nine. On Sundays, birthdays, and a few saints' days, we were free and there were four days' holiday at Christmas and Easter."

That was the way in which Princess Marina's father and uncles were brought up—the hard way in all truth. Little wonder that the heir to the throne bore the title of Duke of Sparta.

Prince Nicholas brought up his daughters not on such Spartan lines, but with plenty of healthy outdoor exercise. An English groom, called Taylor, taught them riding. Princess Marina adored it. She was utterly without fear. Whilst only eight years old she jumped a ditch, against orders—and stuck to the saddle. Taylor gasped.

Another day they were riding in the riding school when Princess Olga's pony ran into a ladder and, as she described it to a friend:

"He started climbing up the steps. That really terrified me."

Most mornings the three Princesses with their three Royal cousins, Prince Philip's two eldest sisters and Princess Helen, rode out with Taylor on their ponies—six laughing little girls whose greatest fun in life was to bolt suddenly from the groom in different directions and then exchange mounts.

"It made Taylor furious," Princess Marina chuckled as she told the story to friends years later.

One day she came back from riding after a hard gallop. Her pony was hot and steaming.

"You must not bring him in like that," her father expostulated, "it's bad for you and bad for the pony to come home hot and tired."

"Don't worry," Princess Marina said coolly. "We have both a good consistency."

Even today in Greece, older people speak with nostalgic affection of the six charming little girls who used to ride by on their ponies laughing and chattering, or drive through the streets in open carriages, waving to the crowds who adored them.

Sometimes they took picnic baskets to the sandy beaches of Phaleron to bathe in the blue waters of the Aegean Sea. Princess Marina learnt to swim at the age of three when she hurled herself into the water without consulting anyone, merely because she saw her elder sisters swimming in it.

Music and the theatre were early loves. All the Greek Royal family were passionately devoted to the theatre and good at acting. Most of them were good musicians as well, particularly Prince Christopher, her uncle, and Prince Paul, her cousin.

Princess Marina took part in a good many private theatricals in her father's own theatre in Athens.

Baroness von der Hoven describes another theatrical occasion at Princess Marina's own home:

"It is ten minutes to eight and the curtain will go up in a few minutes. Prince and Princess Nicholas sit in the first row of the improvised theatre in their own garden. The hall is full of members of the family, statesmen, noblemen and members of the diplomatic corps . . .

"A business-like atmosphere reigns in the dressing-rooms. Everyone has to be on his mettle. Prince Nicholas as producer, gives the last orders, sees to this and that. There's no forgetting of parts, no giggling or getting away with it just because you are a princess and rather beautiful, and in her dressing-room little Princess Marina puts the finishing touches to her make-up, and quivering with impatience like the little thoroughbred she is, is waiting to come on and give of her best, and earn her well-deserved success.

"She has composed most of the dances herself, copying them from the Greek peasant dances which she had seen. She had also trained her little cousins and planned the whole performance. She had ordered about her little troupe; she knew exactly what she wanted and how she wanted it done, and though the youngest of the group, she had to be obeyed. She had worked very hard, guided by the advice of her father whose artistic authority in her eyes was unquestionable."

From that early training sprang that enduring love of music and the theatre which has made her today the patroness of good acting and good music.

CHAPTER THREE

War and the Murdered King

TATOI, IS PERHAPS, the dearest place in the Duchess of Kent's childhood memories. It was the private country estate of her grandfather, King George I of Greece—the Sandringham of the Greek Royal family. Perhaps it would be truer to liken it to Balmoral for it was a paradise of mountains, fir-forests, pine-woods and mountain streams falling like lace.

The house was large, built on the plan and of the style of a good, plain, Georgian English country house. It had a certain Lutyens quality, particularly in the pitch of the roof. A house built squarely, and yet not in a square, since it had bold angles, irregular corners and gables. A house of dignity but not of grandeur.

It stood at the foot of the Parnes Mountains in the north-west of the plain of Attica, about twelve hundred feet above sea-level. A hilly country, splendid with great woods of pine. Acacias, poplars, cypresses and plane trees fringed the roads and sheltered the few houses.

The estate, which King George I bought in 1871, ran to forty thousand acres. Most was forest with a few lowland farms. The present house was built in 1886. It gazed from wide windows across the Attic Plain, glimmering in the sun, to the white-walled city of Athens, twenty-four kilometres away, and the splendour of the glittering sea beyond.

There were orchards, vineyards, a great stockaded deer paddock full of mighty red stags who roared and clashed their antlers, a home farm, stables and nurseries for young trees. In spring the orchards were a coloured sea of apple and cherry blossom, a riot of greengage and quince in ethereal bloom.

The house contained a rather ornate drawing-room and double dining-room with suites of rooms for the various members of the family. These were decorated in a quite simple but charming style. A broad veranda ran along the front of the house with shallow steps leading to a sunny terrace full of flowers and, lower still, a garden.

All about the house and garden stood sentinel belts and clumps of dark cypresses contrasting with the lighter green of plane trees and the darker, cloudy tops of evergreen oaks.

Fifty miles of private roads, built by King George I, climbed the marching miles of grey-green hills, through dim and resinous forests and snaked downhill into the valleys below. Hard by the house itself were vineyards, where the Royal family's own wine was made. The grapes were gathered and stamped out in great vats by the bare feet of peasants. Then there was a home farm, with a dairy, where the pigs and cows ate, rather grandly, out of white marble troughs.

The estate cottages, with their cheerful, bronzed men, each with his fierce moustache, and their bright-faced, smiling women in gaily embroidered skirts, were served by a little shop which stocked everything. Nearby was an enchanting little inn but visitors were not allowed to stay more than a couple of nights. The King, not unnaturally, hated the idea of his private estate, his own little kingdom, being overrun by prying strangers.

Beyond the house and gardens, the home farm and the deer paddock, stretched endless aisles of reddened pines, soaring to the blue sky, seen thinly between their whispering tops. Under the trees lay a thick carpet of pine needles where the little Princesses romped, played hide-and-seek, and had their picnics. That quiet forest, a place of listening stillness, eternal as time, was quick with the stealing feet of red deer and the graceful little roe-deer. There were foxes, reddish-brown, and wild boar, grim and grunting, fearless of man or dog. And sometimes there were the grey and slinking shadows of wolves, the shepherds' nightmare.

On the hills where the forest broke into wastes of grey-green rocks, time seemed to stand still. Pan and the old gods of Ashtaroth had been the spirits of such silent, manless places.

Sometimes the tall red stags came out of the forest into the gardens at night and ate the flowers under Princess Marina's window. Their slot-marks could be seen plainly in the soil and on the lawns at breakfast. And although there were no pheasants, as in English woods, there were great flights of woodcock on migration, owls hooting under the moon, hawks and buzzards sailing in wide sweeps against the ice-blue of the far mountain ridges. Over all lorded the high, bare peaks of Mount Hymettus, stark against the skies of Aegean blue. Prince Nicholas painted one of his best pictures of that view, the bald mountain looming beyond the last outposts of the woodland.

King George was driving Prince Cariatti, the Italian Chargé

d'Affaires, along a forest road one day when a wolf loped out of the forest and followed them for ten minutes, not a hundred yards behind.

When Prince Cariatti was signing his name in the visitors' book before leaving, the King said: "Be sure to say that a wolf followed us. Otherwise no one will believe us!"

Life at Tatoi was free, unfettered and homely. Queen Olga of Greece once said that it was the one place in which she never felt homesick. The Royal children loved it. It was the ultimate Elysium of romps, games, picnics, rides and excursions into the forest. Every cow, pig, donkey and hen had its name.

At night, Princess Marina could hear the great red stags roaring in the forests, the owls hooting, the sharp bark of foxes and sometimes the grunt and squeal of huge, grey-whiskered wild boar, with tusks like knives. They could rip up a man.

Unforgettable and indeed incredible to modern urban minds was the annual fête and midnight feast given on the Queen's birthday and name-day to all the workers, tenants, shepherds, foresters, hunters and trappers on the estate. All were invited with the entire population of a village ten miles away. It was a day of feudal feasting and paternal benevolence, whose like the world will never see again.

The day began with the arrival of a military band from Athens. They marched three times round the house playing a favourite march. After breakfast the children all offered their presents and congratulations. Then the Court ladies and the military and civil household of the palace in Athens arrived by about half-past nine. At ten the Royal family attended a birthday service in the little church of St. Elia which stood on a hill in the wood near the house.

Prince Nicholas describes the scene thus:

"On one side of the steps leading up to the Church stood the small garrison of Tatoi; the gendarmes, and the Evzoni—those picturesque guards so much admired by all visitors to Athens—in their short, white skirts, the fustanella, their red caps with the long, black tassels, white gaiters, and brown leather shoes, with huge pompons, curled up at the front."

When darkness fell over the mountains and the serried lines of soaring pines on the hills stood out like marching armies against the white moon, the great feast started. Hundreds of soldiers, peasants, shepherds and workmen squatted on the grass round table-cloths spread on the ground. Twenty sheep turned and sizzled on enormous spits over blazing fires. It took two hours to roast each sheep.

The soldiers, who ate separately, had their own plates and goblets and used knives and forks, but most of the peasants and workmen used their fingers. They grabbed a piece of hot, sizzling, roast mutton, ate it between finger and thumb and then wiped their hands on the leaves.

The red, resinous Greek wine went round. And there, as Prince Nicholas has described it, were: "all those people, sitting cross-legged, eating their mutton and drinking their wine, as happy as kings, or rather, as kings ought to be.

"My father always went and drank a glass of wine with them, and wished them happiness and prosperity. The senior petty-officer would then answer the toast by another toast to the Queen, expressed in a few hearty words. Whenever my father drank the health of soldiers he always called them 'my children'. The luncheon over, the dance began. They all danced in a chain, as the rustic people love to do, to the weird tune of a kind of hornpipe, whistle and drum. What horrible music! But they played until the poor musicians were blue in the face with heat, and until deep into the night. The peasants had their dance too, in which the women took a prominent part. They had on their best clothes; some of the dresses were of white linen which reached to the ankles, while the others wore short ones made of heavy cloth richly embroidered. Their large vests of white cloth were also em-broidered, and held at the waist by silver clasps; on their heads were yellow, brown, or white kerchiefs printed with coloured flowers.

"When the band was at its hottest and the perspiration was stream-ing from the musicians' faces, my father, following an old custom, used to place a sovereign on every man's forehead, and, the perspira-tion acting as glue, the coins remained safely in position.

"Often when we retired to bed we could hear the primitive music fading away in the distance as the revellers, having danced enough, were returning to their homes. How they enjoyed their King's hospi-tality, and talked of it till the next fête came round again."

Princess Marina and her sisters went among the feasting peasants talking and laughing with them, adored by the women and toasted by the men. Many women brought the little Princesses bunches of flowers, pieces of home-made embroidery.

Those memories of idyllic, far-off days, among an unspoiled people in the mountains, linger today. Sometimes in Kensington Palace, or in the quiet peace of Coppins, the Duchess hears again in memory the wild skirl of the Grecian bagpipes. The drums throbbing through the

dark forest, the old, old, rough music that rang through the mountains and over the isles of Greece when the gods were young.

When Princess Marina was six her father kicked himself playing
tennis. The result, fantastically enough, was a bad attack of phlebitis.
Very soon he was on crutches. So, he went to Bagnoles de l'Orne for a
cure under the admirable Doctor Quiserne, then the greatest vein
specialist in the world.

For three weeks it rained endlessly. The Prince was confined to his
hotel. He recalled that his only companion was a little girl, aged five,
Brenda Van Ellis, the little daughter of a British naval officer. And he
adds:

"Seeing my door open, she peeped in. We became the best of
friends. She paid me daily visits, and when I showed her the photograph of my three little girls, she asked me with a very serious expression, 'Do your babies come from Harrod's stores, because my
Mummy got me there?'

Alas, for such light-hearted interludes. The Prince had no sooner
recovered and rejoined his own little girls than war-clouds darkened
the Greek horizon. Abdul-Hamid, "Abdul the Damned", Sultan of
Turkey, and the most cunning old fox in the Orient, had been plotting
for a long time to recover the lost empire of Islam in the Balkans. He
was the wolf on the doorstep. Then the Young Turk party got rid of
him. Two hundred worse tyrants took his place. Their hatred towards
Greece was far more ruthless and intense than ever had been the plots
and intrigues of Abdul who, rather than go to war, had depended on
shrewd diplomacy to recover the lost lands.

The new Turkish Government proceeded to tax, oppress and torture
the Christian populations of Thrace and Macedonia, nearly all of them
Greek, with appalling ferocity. They refused to listen to reason and
respected nothing but force. All the Balkan states decided at last that it
was time for a final settlement with the common enemy.

Bulgaria and Serbia first declared war on Turkey, Greece followed.
The Crown Prince Constantine, Princess Marina's uncle, took command of the army and in three weeks thrashed the Turks in two great
battles at Sarantaporo and Yanitsa, sweeping over wide plains and
scaling high mountains. It was a terrific stroke of generalship. Any
army could have been proud of that lightning swoop over some of the
roughest country in Europe. War began on October 18th. On November 9th the Greek Army was before the gates of Salonica.

Next day, the Crown Prince at the head of the Army entered the town and was greeted with indescribable, hysterical joy. The Greek population went mad. Some flung themselves in the mud in front of his horse. Others kissed his riding boots and the hem of his greatcoat. Men and women danced, sang, shouted and wept.

Crown Prince Constantine entered the Government Palace where he received the sword of Taxim Pasha.

Next day, King George I of Greece made a triumphal entry into the city on horseback, through streets packed black with people cheering and singing, and lined with troops. It was the supreme moment of his life.

Away in Athens, where Princess Marina played with her sisters, everyone was gay, bright and on top of the world. Dimly the children understood that "Apapa", their beloved grandfather, and Uncle Tino had won a great war.

Soon after came the first fearful blow of tragedy. King George of Greece decided to stay for some considerable time at Salonica. It was the great Macedonian seaport, a proud jewel of ancient Greece. But the Bulgarians, allegedly allies but as cunning as foxes, laid claim to it. Their plan was to make it a divided city as Russia has divided Berlin today. So King George decided to stay there, reign there and rule there on the principle of "What I have, I hold." The Macedonians worshipped him—their saviour from "The Terrible Turk"—the man whose eldest son and army had liberated them after five centuries of appalling slavery.

Eighteen months later came the blow. The Crown Prince had just won another victory at Janina. Princess Marina's father was Military Governor of Salonica. She was at home with her sisters and mother.

The King, her grandfather, had lunch on that fatal 18th day of March, 1913, with Prince Nicholas. He talked happily about the latest victory. He asked Princess Marina's father, even then an outstanding artist, to design a decoration for military valour for the officers and soldiers who had fought so splendidly.

Then the King went out for his daily walk with his A.D.C. He never permitted an armed guard to accompany him. In Athens he walked about the streets alone, chatting with all sorts of people. Why should he fear anyone here in Salonica? The city which his Army had just delivered from five hundred years of Turkish oppression. Day after day, men and women kissed his hand as he walked by. His soldiers were the heroes of the day.

So the King and his A.D.C., chatting together, strode off along a road, their hearts high. Ahead, a low, stone wall topped by iron railings, bordered the road. A man was sitting there. They paid no particular attention to him. He did not rise as the King approached.

Just before they reached the sitting man, the King and his A.D.C. turned smartly about and started to stride back to the city. The waiting man rose from his seat, pulled out a revolver and shot the King in the back. The bullet went clean through his heart. He fell without a word.

The A.D.C. whipped round, jumped on the assassin, knocked the gun out of his hand and handed the murderer over to police who came running at top speed.

A four-wheeled horse-cab pulled up by the roadside. They lifted the tall, soldierly King, the Dane who had given his heart and life for Greece, into the cab and drove him to the Military Hospital.

He was already dead.

Prince Nicholas was in his garden. The first he knew was when a soldier rushed into the garden without warning and stammered through his tears: "They have struck the King. They have taken him to the hospital."

Prince Nicholas, stunned, had the quick mind to announce to the city that the assassin was a Greek although he feared that he was a Bulgarian. The town was full of Bulgarian troops. Bulgars and Greeks loathed each other. Had the rumour run riot that the murderer was a Bulgarian, instant fighting would have broken out between the two armed forces. And "Foxy Ferdinand", the King of Bulgaria, would have seized that excuse to declare war on Greece herself.

Such a shot, fired a year later at Sarajevo, started the First World War. Prince Nicholas's instant decision that day almost undoubtedly prevented war.

It turned out that the assassin was a madman, a Macedonian, a man with a diseased mind, representing no party and no faction.

That afternoon a Fleet Street journalist, Crawford Price, sat down with the haggard Prince Nicholas and wrote out the English telegrams to the dead King's many English relations. Prince Nicholas recorded that he was "a friend in need—a friend indeed".

That night, at eleven o'clock, Princess Marina's grandfather, kindest and best of kings, was placed on a stretcher. The dead King lay in his khaki field uniform, "an expression of peace and happiness upon his face".

A sad procession of officers, many in tears, shouldered the stretcher, tramped through the deadly stillness of the night. Thus the dead King

Her Russian grandparents: Princess Marina (left) with her grandmother, the Grand Duchess Maria Pavlovna, during a holiday visit to Russia; her grandfather, the Grand Duke Vladimir brother of Tsar Alexander III and uncle of the last tsar, Nicholas II

Mother and daughter: Princess Marina at the
age of sixteen and (inset) Princess Alexandra
at the same age

went to his palace. People came to their doors shaking with sobs, holding little lighted candles in their hands. They crossed themselves reverently as their beloved Sovereign was borne past by his officers, their faces white with anguish, tears streaming down their cheeks, their field-boots tramping hollowly.

They took the dead King from Salonica to Athens in the Royal yacht. The streets were lined with troops, their arms reversed. Dense crowds of men, women and children sobbed and wailed.

Behind the coffin, rumbling along on a gun-carriage, marched blue-jackets from the British, Russian and German navies. After them walked deputations of Moslems and Jews. They, too, loved "the Christian King" as they called him.

For a few days the body lay in State in the cathedral in Athens. Then the King, who had done so much for Greece, who had walked among his people as a father and a friend, who had lived, as Princess Marina's father said: "Not only as a king, but, more important, as a gentleman", was taken to Tatoi.

There he lies today, in the tiny churchyard of St. Elias on the little hill. Over his grave the sea-wind sings in the roaring pines where the red deer walk in beauty. He would never have them shot.

At home in the white, sunny house in Athens, Princess Olga asked piteously, again and again, "Where is Apapa? Why don't you take me to see my dear Apapa?"

Each Sunday the three little Princesses had been taken to visit their grandparents when they were in Athens. Even whilst "Apapa" was away they constantly heard from him or of him.

So they told the little girl that "Apapa" had been taken from her. She threw herself on the floor and sobbed bitterly. It was the first cold meeting with death—the first shuddering blow.

Little did her family or the children know that soon were to follow other hammer-blows of fate—cruel, relentless, pitiless.

They were to lose within a few years, their throne, their home, their fortune. Tatoi burned about the King's ears. Themselves slandered, vilified, in the most devilish fashion. Many of their relatives slaughtered like cattle or driven from their homes like criminals. The lights of civilization, the old and gracious civilization, were flickering to a dreadful close. Europe trembled on the edge of anarchy.

King Constantine, Uncle Tino to the Princesses, ascended the throne. He was the hero of his people. The gallant soldier. The liberator of Macedonia. The man who had thrashed the Turks.

3

Tall, dark-haired, commanding, he had his father's kind eyes and strict sense of duty. The fighting blood and sporting courage of his Danish ancestors ran in his veins. He had turned the Greek Army from an ill-disciplined, factious, unorganized force into a fighting army.

The war against Turkey, following hard on the heels of a previous campaign, had, however, squeezed the country hard. The Army had lost many of its best officers. No small army can fight two wars running over roadless mountains, vast swamps and arid plains without suffering in equipment, man-power, fire-power and reserves. The Greek Army needed, and deserved, a rest. So did King Tino. It was not to be.

This is no place to unravel the tangled web of Greek politics. Suffice it to say that the Prime Minister, Venizelos, a brilliant, unstable, ambitious, untrustworthy man, saw himself as the arbiter of the kingdom. All power, he considered, should lie in his hands. Since there had to be a king, let him be a puppet, a figurehead.

That was the philosophy of Venizelos, the arch-plotter with the death's head face, and the spade beard, which made him look like the more successful type of stage villain.

King Tino was a constitutional king. He did not interfere in politics or sway them. But when he found Venizelos trying to swing Greece into another war, he refused to be a party to it. They quarrelled over other matters before this supreme test of strength came to a head, when the 1914 war burst on Europe in a tide of blood.

Less than nine months after the mad murderer rose from his stone wall seat and fired the fatal bullet into King George's back, another shot was fired by another assassin in the little Balkan town of Sarajevo. The Austrian Archduke Franz Ferdinand fell dead. The First World War followed in August, 1914. The cataclysm of blood had begun. The Age of Anarchy came to its first, full, evil flower.

Europe was then governed by three empires and fourteen monarchies. By the end of that war the Russian, German and Austrian empires were shattered. Half a score of monarchies fell or tottered.

France, Britain and Russia demanded that Greece should come in on the side of the Allies. Venizelos, the ready tool of Lloyd George, the Welsh political mountebank, who knew less about European geography and history than the average schoolboy, plunged for war. King Tino stood firm. He was a Greek first—a King—and he knew that his kingdom, weakened by wars, could not afford a second one. He played for time. Who could blame him?

So the campaign of slander began—the campaign which blackened the lives of Princess Marina's parents, lost them their home and fortune and drove them with the children into poverty, obscurity and humiliation.

King Tino, said the sly slanderers, was pro-German. Had he not married the Kaiser's sister? Had he not sent his son, the Crown Prince, years before, to receive his Army training with the Prussian Guards?

The truth was that Queen Sophie of Greece disliked her arrogant, theatrical, Imperial brother intensely. She was perfectly happy in her new country of Greece. Like the Danish-born George I, she became a Greek when Greece became her country.

The fact that the Crown Prince had served with the Prussian Guards was not to his discredit. The German Army then was the military model for the world. If the son of the monarch of a small kingdom wished to learn to be a commander of men in the Continental tradition, the German Army was the obvious training-ground. Equally, if the son of a foreign king wished to become a sailor, the British Navy was the school for him. That was the long and the short of it. But it made a perfect hot-bed of slander and propaganda. Venizelos saw to that.

Princess Marina's family were to suffer bitterly because of the intrigues and overweening vanity of that arch-plotter. Triumph and disaster, murder and exile, waited in the wings of time.

CHAPTER FOUR

The Murder of the Tsar and His Family

THE BALKANS were on the boil. Europe trembled on the verge of the First World War. Princess Marina, then seven years old, went with her sisters to stay with her maternal grandparents, the Grand Duke and Grand Duchess Vladimir of Russia. The Grand Duke was a relative of the last Tsar of Russia. Four years later the Tsar and his family were murdered in a cellar by the Bolsheviks with the most revolting barbarism.

The Grand Duke and Grand Duchess lived partly at the Summer Palace at Tsarskoe Selo and partly in St. Petersburg, now Leningrad.

It was not Princess Marina's first visit to Russia but it was her last trip to fairyland. Tsarskoe Selo, one of the loveliest palaces in Europe, stood near the sea on the Gulf of Kronstadt, a little way from St. Petersburg. It was the epitome of eighteenth-century stateliness, splendid with Doric columns, glittering with tall windows, the long roofs dominated by gilded minarets surmounted by onion-shaped domes which shone like gold in the sun.

The walls of one room were of solid amber. Inset, in panels, were priceless plates of old Chinese porcelain, presented long before to Catherine the Great by the Emperor of China. Their value was beyond computation.

Another room, walled in lapis lazuli, gleamed with the deep blue of Mediterranean skies. The vast banqueting hall, two storeys high, was a poem in blue and silver, lit by thousands of candles. At night, a place of breathtaking beauty.

The furnishings of the Palace had few equals in the world. Gobelin tapestries glowed on the walls. Savonnerie carpets made seas of soft colours on the floors. China from Sèvres, Meissen, and Nymphenburg, with Dubarry tapestries, designed by Boucher, that master of the romantic pastoral, set off the superb Louis XVI furniture in gilt and ormolu. Cabinets of marquetry and intarzia by Roentgen and Risner, with delicate bronzes by Gouthiere for which a collector would have given his ears, were mere incidentals in this treasure-house of art.

Fabergé, the famous Russian Court Jeweller, whose work today is bought by American and international collectors at top prices, was represented by innumerable small gold and jewelled watches, clocks, snuff-boxes, vinaigrettes and other bibelots. The pictures ranged from the luminous Dutch masterpieces of Rembrandt and Aelbert Cuyp, that master of the nuances of sunlight, to the delicate, romantic fantasies of Greuze and Watteau.

Here, under acres of roofs, in lofty rooms of gilt and marble was gathered the fine flower of centuries of civilized art.

A State banquet in the great banqueting hall which extended the entire width of the Palace, was a literal and actual scene from fairyland. Three thousand guests could sit down to dine. The tables glittered with gold plate and the diners glittered with decorations, jewels, silks, satins, uniforms and traditional dresses of almost barbaric splendour.

Each Royal guest was attended by a Court official. He handed the champagne for the toasts. The wine was first poured out by footmen. They passed it to a page. He passed it to the hander. This harked back to medieval days when the pages had to taste the wine to guard against poisoning.

Princess Marina's uncle, Prince Christopher of Greece, recorded that the pages, who were young men of noble family, were highly impressionable. So much so that when Queen Marie of Rumania stayed at the Palace the pages had to be changed every day. They fell in love with her one after the other.

The "hander" of the champagne was usually an aged gentleman with a shaky hand who occasionally managed to upset the wine. Prince Christopher says: "I can still remember my sister's distress when her favourite pale blue velvet Court dress turned a vivid green in patches after her hander had spilt six glasses of champagne over it."

The doorway on these State occasions was sentinelled by the Abyssinian Guard. Six enormous, coal-black negroes in scarlet turbans and wide trousers, with shining scimitars. They stood motionless, the whites of their eyes gleaming uncannily. They had been presented to the Tsar by the Emperor Menelik of Abyssinia—the final touch of pure *Arabian Nights* fantasy.

This, then, was the fairy-tale world to which Princess Marina and her two sisters went with their parents in the summer of 1914. They left the comparative simplicity of their home in Athens for the most splendid and extravagant Court in Europe. A world of barbaric extravagance.

The Tsar was a man of essentially simple tastes but he and his family had inherited pictures, jewels, works of art, magnificent furniture, priceless tapestries and stately palaces which had no equal in the world. Great artists, cunning jewellers, the world's finest designers of furniture, architects of all nations—all had contributed to the splendour and beauty. One can imagine how the eyes of the three little girls from Greece boggled. One wing of the Palace alone would have swallowed their own home in Athens.

It was a great adventure. The children sailed in the Royal yacht from Athens to Sevastopol on the Black Sea, passing through the Dardanelles. Within a few years that narrow seaway echoed with the rolling thunder of guns and saw the heroic assault—and defeat—of British Empire troops on the towering heights defended by Turkey.

Princess Marina and her sisters saw, from the sea, the soaring minarets, the lordly mosques and gleaming palaces of Constantinople, the ancient, all-powerful city of the Byzantine Emperors. For centuries the Turk had stamped Greece and the Balkans under an iron heel. When they landed at Sevastopol, the port of the Crimea, they were on the Riviera of Russia.

The Imperial train waited for them. Court officials in brilliant uniforms bowed Prince and Princess Nicholas and the children on to the train. Their saloons were upholstered in silks and damasks. Their feet sank into thick carpets. In the sleeping compartments were real beds with sheets of fine linen and silken eiderdowns. But the train only travelled at twenty miles an hour. That was the limit of speed for all Imperial trains. So, for days, the three little girls travelled from the far south of Russia through the vineyards and wheat-fields to the endless plains, the marching forests, cold mountains and bleak steppes of the interior. Day after day they gazed from the windows, enchanted.

At each station officials met them with presents of sweets and fruit. It was a Royal Progress.

Little did they realize that, within a few months, they would return in acute discomfort through a country alight with war. They were seeing for the last time, the magnificence of Imperial Russia, the final splendour of a dying age.

Princess Marina's grandparents, the Grand Duke and Duchess, kept their own separate Court. The Grand Duchess had her own Mistress of the Robes, Ladies-in-Waiting and Maids-of-Honour. The Court officials wore magnificent uniforms. Even the pages wore white breeches, gold-braided black coats and black casques with flowing white horsehair.

The Court dresses were medieval. Tight fitting bodices with trains yards long, blazing with jewels. Many jewels were literally priceless. They included emeralds and rubies as big as pigeons' eggs.

Princess Marina played in splendid rooms surrounded by glittering magnificence in a palace which, at night, when chandeliers blazed with a thousand lights, looked unreal, unearthly. She was not over-awed. It was simply "Grandpapa's home". She thanked her grandparents for her lovely presents but, aside, she longed for Mary, that old and slightly battered doll, in Athens.

She and her two sisters were given a suite of rooms with "dear Foxy" to keep a guardian eye on them. There they played with their Russian cousins, the son and daughters of the Tsar, the little Tsarevich Alexis and the two small Grand Duchesses, Anastasia and Marie. Four years later those children were shot like dogs by the Communists.

The little Tsarevich could not, however, play any normal games. The slightest cut or scratch might have meant death. For years the Tsarina had prayed for a son and heir. Then she had given birth to a son who inherited from her own family, the Hesse-Darmstadts, the dreadful scourge of haemophilia. It meant that even a graze could bring on a terrible haemorrhage.

It was said that Bismarck, the cold, calculating "Iron Chancellor" of Germany, knowing of this hereditary scourge, had encouraged the marriage, hoping thus to wipe out the Romanoff dynasty of Russia and enable Germany to conquer Russia!

During those first visits to Russia, Princess Marina's small cousins often saw one of the most evil figures in modern history—a tall, sinister-looking monk with a goat's beard and enormous, magnetic eyes. At the sight of this shambling creature with the burning eyes the little Grand Duchesses would cease playing and kneel devoutly. The monk blessed them and passed on.

"It is the Staretz," (the Holy Man), they said, reverently.

This was Rasputin, the monk. Next to the Tsar he was the most powerful man in all Russia.

That incarnation of vice was then at the top of his power. No man in the last hundred years has exercised such diabolical influence on a monarch.

Born on July 7th, 1872, in a tumbledown hut in the remote village of Pokrovskoie near Tobolsk in Siberia, Gregory Effimovitch was the son of a drunken horse-thief, nicknamed "Rasputin" which means "corrupt". That name descended to his son—as big a drunken blackguard as his father.

This ignorant lout became, in a few years, a "Holy Man". He practised conjuring, sleight of hand and common or garden "magic". This, added to his compelling manner, piercing eyes and carefully cultivated air of mysticism rapidly made him the rage in the aristocratic world of St. Petersburg. Russians of all classes were riddled with superstition and religious mania.

Rasputin, introduced to the Tsarina, announced that he could cure her son. That gave him immediate and immense power. The Empress —and the Emperor—became his devoted disciples.

Miss Meriel Buchanan, daughter of the then British Ambassador to Russia, Sir George Buchanan, told me that Rasputin, utterly vicious in private life, had undoubted hypnotic powers of healing. This first came to the notice of the two "Black Grand Duchesses", the King of Montenegro's daughters, who married the Grand Dukes Nicholas and Peter. They introduced him to the Tsarina. When Rasputin was at Court, the Tsarevitch was reasonably well. If the Monk left, he became worse. If Rasputin wrote or telephoned, the child instantly improved.

This macabre liar, forger and swindler, hated by most Russians, frequently warned the Tsar: "If anything happens to me, the Russian Empire will crumble. My death means your death." He begged the Tsar not to declare war in 1914. It would ruin Russia. Later, he said to the French Ambassador, M. Paléologue: "For twenty years nothing but blood and sorrow will be reaped on Russian fields."

This then, was the sinister power who influenced the amiable Tsar and his haughty, German-born Tsarina. Two years later Rasputin died. Prince Youssoupoff and his friends, the Grand Duke Dimitri Pavlovitch and Pourichkievitch, a Conservative member of the Duma, the Russian Parliament, killed him.

They gave him a poisoned drink containing cyanide of potassium. He gulped it down—and asked for another. They put three bullets into him. He still breathed. They hit him on the head with an iron bar and threw him into the ice-jammed River Neva. He was still alive when he hit the water!

Days later his body was found. Thus died the embodiment of all evil.

Luckily Princess Marina knew nothing of the monk's appalling power for evil. She was too young.

Her young and beautiful grandmother, the Grand Duchess Vladimir, fascinated and enchanted her. Her grandmother was a great leader of Society, a woman of wide sympathy and great good taste. Round her she gathered brilliant writers, painters, and musicians. Her Court was not only splendid and impressive but full of brains.

When Princess Marina saw her in medieval, regal splendour, glittering in jewels, in her Court dress with its long train, wearing on her head the kokoschnik, the traditional head-dress of the Imperial Court, glowing with enormous sapphires, she clapped her hands delightedly and said:

"May I put it on?"

The Grand Duchess, laughing, took the kokoschnik from her head and placed it on Princess Marina's hair. The child, bubbling with delight, studied herself in a long looking-glass.

"Can't I have one too?" she asked.

"Of course you will, when you're grown up."

Within four years the Grand Duchess was a hunted exile, Princess Marina a child in exile too—with a Royal coronet of England waiting for her down the years.

That enchanted summer, spent playing among the glowing flower beds, the rolling lawns and stately trees of the park surrounding Tsarskoe Selo, was the last time she saw Russia.

There came a bright morning in 1914. Their parents, looking strained and worried, took the children from the Palace to the train. They drove to St. Petersburg where endless columns of soldiers tramped behind blaring bands. Flags fluttered from every building and flagpole. Always the marching men, the prancing horses, the pennoned lances, the rumbling cannon, the tramp, tramp, tramp of endless feet.

They were put on the train with the watchful eye and capable English hands of Miss Fox, their governess, tending them with hawk-like care.

This time the train was hot, crowded and stuffy. It rumbled southwards through towns and by villages where flags flew and men were on the endless march. Time and again the train was shunted into sidings whilst troop trains thundered past. Hour after hour they spent waiting for the trains that were taking men to the war. The Tsar of All the Russias was summoning his armies.

It was lucky that their parents, Prince and Princess Nicholas, were with the children in those fateful days. They left Russia on August 28th, twenty-seven days after Germany had declared war on Russia. Before they left, the Tsar told Princess Marina's father how desperately anxious he was to avoid war, how much he feared the Kaiser's plan for domination of Europe.

Nicholas II, Tsar of Russia, was the double in appearance of George V of England. It was almost impossible to tell them apart. Like George V he was merry, good-humoured, and above all, a lovable man. He liked simple food and simple pleasures. Elaborate ceremonies secretly bored him but he never showed it. He had great natural dignity when the occasion demanded. He was deeply religious, acutely conscious of his enormous burden of moral, spiritual and temporal power as "The Little Father of All the Russias", the Lord's Anointed as head of the Russian Church. The children never saw their gentle, beloved uncle again.

Owing to the war, King Carol I of Rumania sent a special train to meet Prince Nicholas and his family. It took them from Jassy to Sinaia where they stayed near Queen Elizabeth of Rumania—whom all Europe knew as Carmen Sylva—at the Crown Prince's enchanting little palace of Pelichor, set in a forest of fir-trees.

Carmen Sylva, an imposing and romantic figure in flowing white robes and snow-white hair, spoke the most fluent English and could write English verse and prose with elegance. She was an absolute Fairy Godmother to Princess Marina and her two sisters whom she adored.

When they left, the Crown Prince and Princess of Rumania travelled with them for part of the way. The children were becoming fidgety by the time they reached the port where they had to wait for a boat to cross to Serbia. So the Crown Princess gathered them in a ring round her and told fairy stories which she invented one after another.

The journey through Serbia was, as Prince Nicholas records, "far from pleasant. The heat was unbearable, we had no water and the children cried, until at a railway station we were able to purchase a water-melon with which to quench their thirst."

Baroness von der Hoven tells of the one amusing episode on that journey. She says:

"When they reached the frontier between Serbia and Bulgaria, it was discovered that their luggage had gone astray. Those who were responsible for it rushed about distractedly trying to locate the missing servants, who had been lost together with the things, but the three little princesses throroughly enjoyed themselves when bed-time came and grown-up nighties were produced for them by some obliging strangers.

"Those garments were not exactly of the Paris model type, and raised peals of laughter when one of the three sisters simply disappeared in its voluminous folds or tripped over its trailing hem.

"Princess Marina picked up her 'outsize' robes and performed a dance all over the floor to the delight of her sisters and to the exasperation of her elders, who would gladly have their three little charges settled for the night. This was soon done, however, as the little girls were tired after their long journey.

"The next day proved a real trial and Princess Marina says she remembers the heat and the flies and the long dreary day and eventually the water-melon which was so good!

"At Salonika another halt was made and there they visited the monument erected to their grandfather, King George I, by his widow, Queen Olga. This upset them very much as the little girls had not yet become accustomed to the loss of their 'dear apapa', the handsome old King whom they had loved so much. But returning home to their familiar surroundings in Athens they forgot their sorrows, and especially when they were sent to the villa at Kiffissia they turned again to normal life."

The late Admiral Mark Kerr, whom I knew well, was then Chief of the British Naval Mission in Greece and Commander-in-Chief of the Grecian Navy. A shrewd, kindly man with a twinkling eye, who adored children. He knew the political and international situation inside-out. Had he not been a sailor he could have been a statesman.

He told me once, at dinner, how he had taken Princess Marina and her two little sisters for a short cruise aboard his flagship, the *Averoff*. Princess Marina particularly wanted to see "a real gun". So the Admiral took her into a gun-turret and let her pull the trigger of a six-pounder—unloaded.

He said that her English, even then, was quite word-perfect, but she had difficulty in pronouncing the word "gun". None the less she went on "firing" it for at least ten minutes! He described her as very bright, intensely eager to learn everything and with a mischievous sense of humour. She and her sisters had luncheon and tea in his cabin and, by the time they left the ship, had captured everyone's hearts.

Meanwhile, the Great War raged beyond the frontiers of Greece. All Europe between the Baltic and the Pyrenees was swept into the holocaust.

The Greek Government voted at the outset for neutrality. King Constantine, little Princess Marina's uncle, knew the weaknesses of his Army. He supported his Government. A brilliant soldier with a resounding list of victories to his personal credit against that ancient enemy, the Turk, he knew that his Army was in no fit state to be ground between the upper and nether millstones of a world war.

Venizelos, the Greek Premier, that piratical opportunist who was a mixture of Turk, Armenian and Jew, was determined to curry favour with the Allies in order to advance his own power in Greece. He pulled every string to force Greece into war, to undermine the King, to slander the Queen.

Long past were the days when this cross-bred son of a prosperous carpenter, had gone to the Palace to beg an audience, to tell the previous King, George I, that he was the one person capable of forming a strong Cabinet. That was in the stormy year of 1898 when Greece was having fearful trouble in Crete. Prince Christopher of Greece says of him in those days that he:

". . . appeared out of the blue, a shabby young man with a fox-like smile and an amazing gift of oratory and a still greater gift of putting other people in his pocket. He could talk so convincingly that even my father, though diametrically opposed to many of his theories, had to admit that, after listening to him for an hour, he generally found himself being reluctantly convinced. He was never forceful or compelling; he was smooth as silk, gentle, obsequious with a mind as agile as a rapier and a never-failing flow of words. On brains less alert he had a hypnotic effect; he could sway crowds in whatever direction he wished and twist cabinets this way and that until they did not know their own minds." It all sounds very like the late and unlamented Lloyd George!

Prince Christopher adds: "He was so poor in those days that he wore cracked boots and frayed trousers. His smart frock-coat, he told us afterwards, had been borrowed for the occasion. But there was about him a certain unconscious dignity, the marks of a dominant personality. Underneath his silken urbanity one glimpsed an iron will and an absolute ruthlessness. He was the born political adventurer, piratical and opportunist."

One more sidelight on this man. King Constantine was warned against him time and again. Yet, oddly enough, he liked Venizelos. He even trusted him. Once a Greek statesman showed King Constantine a letter in which Venizelos had openly threatened the King.

"I have kicked out one George already and I've come to Athens to kick out another," he wrote in that damning letter.

The next morning Venizelos went to the Royal Palace in Athens for an audience with the King. What happened is best told in Prince Christopher's own words:

"Before he left my father told him casually that he wanted to show him something, and put the letter in his hand. For once his extraordinary aplomb deserted him. Every vestige of colour went out of his face. 'What are you going to do?' he stammered. My father shook his head: 'Nothing. Take that letter; I give it to you as proof of my faith, for, in spite of it, I trust you.'

"He trusted him to the bitter end."

There is no doubt that Venizelos was financed in his political campaigns by that man of mystery, Sir Basil Zaharoff, whom I personally met more than once. A man of unknown origin, he had neat charm, undoubted culture of a real sort and an uncanny flair for making millions and breaking or making Governments. Probably no man not occupying a governmental position has wielded such behind-the-scenes power in the last 100 years.

That is the picture of the man, who, above all others, ruined the Greek Royal family for more than twenty tortured years. Thereby he changed the whole tenure of Princess Marina's own life.

Whilst the Great War was being fought on the Western Front and in the Polish marshes, with the thunder of guns, the hideous squalor of the trenches and the pathetic chivalry of the last cavalry, life went on in Athens very much the same for Princess Marina and her sisters. Greece was not yet at war.

Outwardly their child-world was the same.

The same games in the garden of the big, square, white house in Athens. The same lessons. Greek grammar and arithmetic which she abominated. Drawing, literature and history which she loved. Picnics in the forest up in the hills at Tatoi, the beloved place. Visits to the little country villa at Kiffissia. The usual family luncheons when all the aunts, uncles and cousins gathered together at the Royal Palace and then again at Prince Nicholas's own house. They were an utterly united, devoted family, with a patriarchal sense of unity.

They were all deeply religious under their gaiety, their bubbling sense of humour. Princess Marina and the other children were brought up by their mother, Princess Nicholas, and by their aunt, Queen Sophie, to believe that whatever happened was the will of God. If ill befell, it must be accepted. God was mightier than the mis-doings of man. Sooner or later, good would triumph over evil. That sound, wise philosophy was to succour them all too soon.

In spite of the games, the lessons and the family luncheons, Princess Marina's quick, sensitive child-mind, realized that things were not as they had been. She was no longer allowed to read the newspapers. Courtiers and servants suddenly broke off conversation when she was within earshot. The word "war" was too often heard. She wondered what it all meant. Her uncle, King Constantine, and her father, both looked haggard, worried. Her aunt, Queen Sophie, was often in tears.

Meanwhile Venizelos, using all the arts of propaganda, publicity and a personally controlled Press, whipped up popular resentment against the King and Queen. It must be remembered that the Greeks were, and are, a southern race—emotional, hot-blooded, easily stirred. Three-quarters of the peasants and poorer townspeople were illiterate. It was the same in every Balkan country, in Russia, in Poland, Spain and elsewhere.

The Greeks, with their long tradition of subservience to the Turks, their mountain-clan feuds, their hatred of Bulgaria, their fear of Germany, their pride in their new independence, were ready fuel for the fires of treachery kindled by Venizelos.

He started the foul slander that Queen Sophie, at her country house of Tatoi, high up in the pine-forests and the mountains, had a secret cable laid which sent news to German submarines. A fantastic lie. But it was enough.

One night when the children were in bed in the little villa at Kiffissia, they suddenly saw out of the bedroom windows a crimson glow in the sky. Far across the dusky plain, high above the olive-groves, against the starlit tapestry of an indigo evening sky, the red glow rose in flickering malevolence. That way, at the feet of Mount Hymettus, lay their beloved Tatoi—their own especial home, set amid its 40,000 acres of pine-forests and rocky hillsides where the goats gambolled, the tall red deer walked in beauty against the skyline. There they knew every cow, donkey, goat, chicken and duck by its own pet name. The forest was on fire!

King Constantine and Queen Sophie were in the great, English-looking Georgianized house at Tatoi that night when the hirelings of Venizelos fired the forest.

But for the fact that the house was ringed by cypresses and evergreen oaks, which do not burn easily—that and the belt of meadowlands and gardens round the house—the King and Queen and their youngest child, Princess Katherine, a babe in arms, would have been burnt alive.

Luckily, King Constantine, brought up to know every shepherd's track, farm road and deer-run on the place, was able to escape. He was fire-fighting at one point when he and his party were almost ringed with flame. He remembered a goat track through the forest which might still be safe. He ran for it, shouting for the others to follow. Alas, many had already bolted to other paths to find each a wall of flame. Sixteen people were burned alive. The King escaped with his young son Paul—the present King Paul of the Hellenes—by racing down the goat-track with flames leaping at them from either side. A race with death through an inferno. They escaped by seconds. Prince Christopher had a near squeak too. Queen Sophie had to run for two miles carrying her baby girl.

Behind them the forest was a blazing inferno. Giant pine-trees, flaming in unearthly splendour, exploded like cannon or crashed to the ground in a shower of sparks that leapt upwards to the mocking skies.

Nearly thirty thousand acres—more than forty square miles—of forest, hillside, farmland and vineyard was wiped out before the fire burnt out. The house was left, smoking, blackened and a mockery. Later, empty petrol cans were found on the forest verge at three different places!

Not one man on the estate had any part in that crass, criminal act. The hirelings of Venizelos had done their work.

Then riots broke out in Athens. Many were for the King. They and the King's enemies fought in the streets, sniped from the rooftops. And to the simple people of Greece, the vast majority, it was all a tragic puzzle, a ghastly mystery. That was how Princess Marina and her sisters saw it also.

"Why are they fighting?" she asked her governess, Miss Fox.

"Some of them are fighting for the King and some against him."

"But why? Why?" the child demanded, again and again.

She threw back her heart-shaped little face, the hair swept back over her right temple, a plain lace collar about her throat, and stared with those direct, amber, green-rimmed eyes, at "dear Foxy". "They all love Uncle Tino so much. Why have they changed like this?"

Alas, it was more than even the level brain and motherly kindliness of the wise "Foxy" could explain.

The end came. The Allies had control of the Greek Navy. Venizelos had the bit between his teeth. Greece was drummed into war whether she wanted it or not. Guns boomed from the ships out in the Piraeus. Shells flew whining over the square white house where the bougain-villeas and oleanders spilled their beauty. One fell by the Palace itself. The children crouched, fearful, in the cellars. War can be very terrify-ing when you are only ten.

King Constantine bowed to inevitable forces. The Allies and Veni-zelos demanded his abdication. He refused. But he agreed to leave Greece. "I am going away for a little while," he announced simply. The soldier who had won two wars was not going to plunge his country into civil war. Nor would he abdicate to please the man who had come to his father long ago with a foxy smile, cracked boots and a borrowed frock-coat, from no-one knew quite where.

Few people know today that Venizelos was the man who allowed the two German warships, the *Goeben* and *Breslau*, to be coaled in a Greek port whilst the British Fleet was in hot pursuit. Greece was then neutral.

The two warships reached Constantinople and threatened to bom-bard the city unless Turkey declared war against the Allies. That act gave Germany her footing in Turkey. It extended the war into Meso-potamia and the Middle East. It cost us the supreme sacrifice—and defeat—of the Dardanelles.

The late Sir Basil Thompson, in his brilliant book *The Allied Secret Service in Greece* exposed this all-too-little-known fact.

"Thereby," said Sir Basil, "Venizelos laid upon his shoulders a heavier responsibility for the miseries of the nations than is borne by any man living except the ex-Kaiser."

This was the man who hounded King Constantine of Greece from his throne.

The King's departure from Athens was one of the most dramatic and pathetic episodes in modern history.

With his country blockaded by Allied ships; Greece's railways, telegraphs and post offices under Allied control and censorship and with the Franco-British Secret Police operating throughout the country, the King was in the abyss of humiliation.

The Venezelists even put it about that he plotted to attack the Allied Forces under General Sarrail in the rear. There was not a word of truth in it.

Lord Kitchener visited Athens and had a long discussion with the King. The latter recorded in his diary:

Wedding group at Buckingham Palace: (left to right) King George V, Princess Nicholas of Greece, Princess Marina and the Duke of Kent, Queen Mary, and Prince Nicholas of Greece; in front, Princess Elizabeth (now Queen Elizabeth II) and Lady May Cambridge (photograph by Bassano)

Leaving for the honeymoon: the Duke and Duchess of Kent at Paddington on their way to Himley Hall

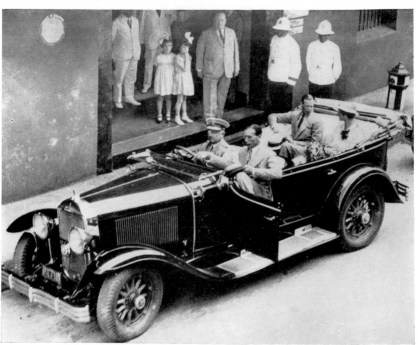

Later in the honeymoon—on tour at Nassau in the Bahamas

"It was a pleasure talking to him and having that comfortable feeling that whatever one said would be given its real meaning and not twisted about and misconstrued as it so often happens when I talk to diplomats. The very first thing I asked him was if he really believed that I was capable of stabbing General Sarrail's army in the back; he laughed outright and said that he had never believed such nonsense, which could only be 'credited' by nervous newspaper correspondents who tried to justify the inactivity of the expeditionary forces."

Kitchener, himself, recorded in his terse way that he could talk to King Constantine as one soldier to another with perfect freedom and understanding. He, above all men, loathed politicians.

Sir Thomas Cunninghame, British Military Attaché at Salonika, said at the time: "The Greek Army saves, and secures, the flanks and the rear of the Allies."

In spite of these vindications of the King the Allied Powers, egged on by Venizelos whom Lloyd George trusted implicitly, sent a special High Commissioner to Greece, Monsieur Jonnart, a smug *bourgeois* Frenchman with a square head and hair *en brosse*, to demand the King's abdication. Jonnart added the threat that if he did not go Athens would be bombarded.

The King decided to go. He did not abdicate. He appointed his younger son, Alexander, to reign in his place. Prince Nicholas wrote in his diary:

"As soon as the Powers' ultimatum and its acceptance by the King became known, confirming their worst suspicions, the people came hurrying to the Palace from every direction. Alarm and dismay were written on every face, and they firmly decided to prevent the King from going away. All the church-bells began to toll mournfully, and the whole town was plunged in despair.

"The Palace was surrounded on all sides, and the soldiers of the King's bodyguard—his faithful Evzoni—received orders to close the gates and to allow no one to enter. The crowds were so thickly massed outside and peremptorily, almost angrily, forbade the exit of anyone who wished to leave the Palace."

It amounted to this. The King was besieged in his own palace by his own people—not in anger but in sorrow. Not to force him from the throne but to keep him on it.

Prince Christopher, Princess Marina's uncle, records his impressions of that pathetic moment.

4

"As the hours passed our plight became dangerous for the lamentations turned to hysteria and there were cries of—'It would be better to kill the King than let him leave Greece', cries isolated at first but after a while caught up and echoed by hundreds. Finally, a ruse was decided upon."

The rumour was started that the King would leave by a back gate. Cars were sent there. The crowd rushed round, screaming that if they could not have the King alive they would keep his corpse among them!

Then Prince Christopher and the others hurried the King and Queen Sophie, who was ill, out by another gate. He wrote:

"We could hear the wooden railings cracking and a general stampede back to the front of the Palace, but by that time the King, Queen Sophie and their children, had hurled themselves unceremoniously into the cars. The Crown Prince drove off lying on the floor of one with his legs waving wildly out of the open door. . . ."

A stunned silence fell over the crowd . . . then the sky darkened suddenly and heavy rain began to fall. This was so rare in a Greek summer that the crowd, superstitious at any time, said it was a bad omen. Several tried to commit suicide on the spot. One man pulled out a revolver. He put it to his head and was about to pull the trigger when a guard knocked it from his hand.

The Royal family reached Tatoi that night. Next day they were besieged by hundreds of weeping subjects. Minister and Society leaders arrived in cars. Workmen came in packed lorries. Peasants trundled up in their wooden country carts. Farmers rode up on horseback, city workers on bicycles.

They crowded round the King in the garden. They knelt at his feet. They begged him to stay. They were, says Prince Christopher, "like bewildered children. It was impossible to make their simple minds realize that he was only leaving them for their own good."

The King and Queen and their children drove from Tatoi to the little waterside village of Oropos on the Gulf of Euboea. It had one small wooden landing stage about fifty feet long. When the Royal family arrived the village and the beach were packed with people. The pier was strewn with flowers. The King and Queen could only advance, step by step, towards the pier.

Princess Marina's father, Prince Nicholas, wrote:

"The crush became even greater when we advanced along the pier —the nearer the King and Queen drew to the boat the fiercer grew the frenzy of the people who tried to keep him back by force. Many leaped into the sea and held fast to the boat.

"The King and Queen, after a last handshake left and right, stepped into the boat. The rest of us followed with difficulty. Among lamentations and sobs that rent the air the boat set slowly off whilst all the people went down on their knees and stretched out their hands towards the King and Queen. It was a heartrending picture."

Prince Nicholas and his family saw the King and Queen on board the *Sphacteria*, a small steamer which had formerly been used as a Royal yacht. There they said good-bye to the King and Queen. In his own words: "The bitter moment of parting had come at last and we were all anxious to end the ordeal as quickly as possible . . . we returned on shore and drove back to Athens. When we reached the top of the hill we looked back to have a last glimpse of the *Sphacteria* as she was steaming out on her way to Italy."

Ten days after the King's expulsion Venizelos entered Athens guarded by foreign troops. Machine-guns were posted along the roofs. That was the measure of his popularity with the Greeks.

King Constantine's younger son, Prince Alexander, ascended the Throne. A lonely, sad young man, a mere puppet, forbidden to speak even to his uncles and cousins. The prisons were filled within a few days with his father's friends.

Soon after Prince Nicholas and his entire family, including Princess Marina, were ordered to leave Greece. Prince Andrew followed a fortnight later. Young King Alexander was left alone, forlorn on a mockery of a throne.

It was Princess Marina's first taste of exile, the first bitter upheaval of her family and home.

She was ten years old in that June of 1916. Tragedy dogged her family remorselessly for the next few bitter years.

CHAPTER FIVE

First Exile—Switzerland

THE MOMENT Princess Marina's family left Athens their private income stopped. They went to St. Moritz. There they lived in a flat with little money. Their Greek servants followed them into exile, served for a time without pay. They worked for love alone. Months went by without any wages being paid. They never complained.

Prince Nicholas and Prince Christopher had to live on borrowed money. The latter said: "An unpleasant test to apply to one's friends, but people were amazingly kind. Just when we were wondering where in the world the next quarter's rent was coming from, someone always stepped into the breach."

Worse, both the Royal brothers were treated as spies and dangerous characters. Secret police dogged them. Their conversations were listened to, reported on. Special agents were told off to spy on them. Their names were on the black list of the Allied Legations.

The worst blow of all came to Princess Marina when her adored governess, "dear Foxy" that devoted Englishwoman with the gold pince-nez, the piled-up hair-do, the high lace collar and the heart of abounding kindness, was sent for one day by the British Consulate. There she was cross-questioned. She was asked to repeat the private conversations of Prince Nicholas and his family. She was told that she would get into terrible trouble if she continued to serve "the traitors of England".

"Foxy" stoutly denied that Prince Nicholas and his family were traitors to this country. She declared that they were victims of the Venizelists' campaign of slander. She was told instantly that unless she gave in her notice she would lose her passport.

Poor "Foxy" went straight back to Prince Nicholas, burst into tears, and told him what had happened. He told her that she would have to go as he did not wish her to get into further trouble on his account.

It was a bitter moment in the nursery when "Foxy" came to tell Princess Marina and her two sisters that she was going home to England, leaving them. There were tears. But "Foxy" stoutly declared: "I shall come back to you, my dears." And she did.

Meanwhile, in Russia, Princess Marina's grandmother, the Dowager Queen Olga of Greece, had a dramatic escape from almost certain death. She had gone to Russia early in the war to open a military hospital at Pavlovsk, a family palace not far from Tsarskoe Selo, the Tsar's Summer Palace. When the Bolshevik Revolution broke a detachment of Red soldiers and sailors was sent to Pavlovsk.

They arrived in the palace at night. Queen Olga was asleep. Her maid, a Russian woman, nearly seventy years of age, stood in front of her mistress's door and said fiercely to the Communist troops:

"You ought to be ashamed of yourselves. Her Majesty has come here to help you—to nurse the wounded. I recognize several of you that she was kind to when you came to Greece on Russian warships. Get out of it now. I won't allow you to disturb her. Be off!"

Quelled by one fierce old woman who knew more than one of them by name and let fly with language which would not have disgraced a sergeant-major, they slunk out.

A few days later a Red mob stormed the palace and sacked it. Queen Olga was lucky to escape with her life. She was even luckier to escape with her jewels.

Her Lady-in-Waiting, Miss Baltazzi, organized a highly ingenious piece of smuggling. She arranged for a Greek student to call with a package of books in a rough wooden box. As he entered the house a Red sentry challenged him, examined the box and, seeing that it contained only books, kicked it contemptuously and told him to go in.

An hour later the student came out again with the same rough wooden box under his arm. This time it was packed with jewels— diamonds, rubies, sapphires, ropes of pearls and one magnificent set of emeralds. The sentry glanced at the shabby student with his wooden box and said contemptuously:

"Pass, comrade."

The jewels were taken straight to the Danish Legation and sent to Copenhagen. Without them the Dowager Queen of Greece would have been penniless.

The Danish Government, with great difficulty, arranged for Queen Olga to leave Russia eventually. That last journey out of the land of terror was nearly her last. She travelled with her Lady-in-Waiting and two maids in a special carriage attached to the end of a train full of German prisoners-of-war who were being repatriated.

On the way to the frontier it stopped at a wayside station. Queen Olga was woken by voices under the windows of her sleeping compartment. She took no notice, thinking they were railway officials, and dropped off to sleep again.

Next morning she was astonished to find that her carriage had been put into the centre of the train for safety.

The men she had heard during the night were Communists. They had tried to uncouple her carriage and leave it on the line. The express was due ten minutes later!

Far worse happened to Princess Marina's maternal grandmother, the Grand Duchess Vladimir. When the Revolution broke she was running a hospital in the Caucasus. The house in which she lived was raided twenty-two times by Communists. Twice she fled into the mountains. The first time she escaped in the middle of the night in nothing but a dressing-gown.

Finally, General Wrangel, the White Russian commander who was fighting a desperate, heroic, back-to-the-wall campaign against the Reds, told her that he could no longer guarantee her safety. He put her and the other refugees in a train for Novorossisk on the Black Sea. The Grand Duchess, racked with illness, frozen with cold, spent seven weeks on that train, living mainly on black bread and soup, cooped up in a tiny compartment with the most primitive sanitary arrangements. The whole place stank.

Finally, she and the other refugees escaped on an Italian steamer. She landed at Venice, travelled to Paris and arrived there with only the clothes she wore.

Here entered that unknown, un-honoured hero of the Russian Revolution, the late Bertie Stopford. He was the typical charming devil-may-care, mildly elegant type of well-bred Englishman who, down the centuries, has quite casually made history. His family, the head of which is the Earl of Courtown, has produced an unfailing crop of admirals, generals, colonial administrators, parsons and gay young men addicted to pig-sticking, polo and poking their noses into dangerous places. Bertie Stopford was a devoted friend. So much so that when Russia was, as Prince Nicholas described it, "a hell-pit" he took his courage in both hands and travelled three times to the Caucasus and back. He was a cross between the Scarlet Pimpernel and Fitzroy Maclean.

When he found that the Grand Duchess was utterly destitute, he calmly announced that he would go to Petrograd and collect her jewels! Somehow by an epic of daring, the whole of which has never been told fully, he got into her Palace in Petrograd disguised as a workman. He opened the safe with the help of a devoted servant, wrapped the jewels in bits of newspaper and stuffed them away in two old Gladstone bags. Then he shuffled out of the Palace in his grimy working clothes and went to the British Embassy. Then he smuggled them through to London. Without those jewels the Grand Duchess would have been utterly destitute.

That story represents only one of the many fantastic hairsbreadth escapes that lit with bright heroism those dark and bitter days of murder.

Many of Princess Marina's relatives were not so lucky. Her aunt the Grand Duchess Elizabeth, a grand-daughter of Queen Victoria, was murdered with the utmost cold-blooded barbarity.

Before the Revolution, her husband, the Grand Duke Serbe, Governor of Moscow, was murdered by a Nihilist. Yet the Grand Duchess, young, delicately featured, heart-broken, had the forgiveness of spirit to ask the Tsar to spare the life of the young student who had thrown the bomb which blew her husband to bits.

In spite of her efforts he was executed—quite rightly. She went to see him in prison before he died. There she promised to look after his mother. She sent the murderer's mother enough money to keep her in comfort until her death.

This noble-spirited woman retired to a convent after the murder of her husband, the Grand Duke. There she lived quietly until the Revolution. Then the Communists sacked the convent, dragged her out and sent her to prison in Siberia with others of the Imperial family.

One morning the Red Guards entered the cell where they were all herded together like animals.

"Get ready. You're going on a journey," they ordered.

"Where to?" the Grand Duchess asked, hoping that they were being sent back to St. Petersburg.

"Somewhere far away," one of the guards answered evasively.

The prisoners, men and women, were made to walk in single file through the snow. Presently this macabre procession came to a dark, yawning pit. The mouth of a disused mine-shaft. When the first prisoner reached the edge of the pit the pathetic little party was ordered to stop.

Two soldiers sprang forward. They seized the leading prisoner, one of the Grand Dukes, and hurled him into the pit. Another, and another, were thrown down. A shuddering minute of time between each. The wretched survivors had to stand and watch this ghastly travesty of an execution.

The Grand Duchess Elizabeth began to sing a hymn. The others, with quavering voices, joined her. One after another their starved and weakened bodies were sent hurtling into the pit. Her turn came. She asked only that she might cover her head with her cape so that she could not see the pit as she was thrown into it. Then this frail woman who had pensioned the mother of her husband's Red murderer, was picked up and sent hurtling down the mine.

Weeks later, Admiral Koltchak's White Army which, with General Wrangel of the other White Army, was fighting a brilliant, but despairing, rearguard action against the Communists, found the mangled bodies at the bottom of the pit. Some were pathetically bandaged with strips of linen torn from their underclothes. Clearly, they had lived for some days in agony, with broken arms and legs, at the bottom of that pit of slime and blackness, before dying.

The slaughter of the Tsar, the Tsarina, the three little Grand Duchesses and the Tsarevich, a weak and sickly boy, on the night of July 16th–17th, 1918, in the cellar of a small and filthy house at Ekaterinburg is one of the blackest crimes in the world's history. Before the murder the Imperial Family, guarded by foul-smelling Letts and jeering Jews, under the murderer, Yankel Yourovski, were subjected to every bestial insult. The young girls had to sleep on the floor. The Red Guards watched them undress and threw filthy remarks at them. They stole their clothes and jewels. The food was nauseating.

Finally, on the night of July 16th, Yankel Yourovski threw open the cellar door. He stamped in with a squad of murderous-looking soldiers.

"Stand up!" he shouted.

The Tsar, his wife and family, stumbled to their feet. The Tsar, sensing what was to come, braced himself and looked them in the face. The children clung to him. They stood for an instant.

Then the rifles crashed out.

The Tsar of All the Russias, cousin of King George V of England, his wife, little girls—one of whom had been frequently mentioned as a possible wife for the Prince of Wales—and the pathetic son, sagged to the ground. A welter of blood and spattered brains.

Letts and Jews leapt on the bodies and hacked them to pieces. The ghastly remains were taken to a secret place in the forest. A great fire of pine branches was lit and the bleeding remnants tossed on it.

"The world will never know what we have done to them," Vaikoff, one of the butchers, boasted proudly.

The late Miss Meriel Buchanan (Mrs. Knowling) with whom I corresponded frequently, who was daughter of Sir George Buchanan, the last British Ambassador to the Tsar, lived through all this ghastly period. She said in her book, *Dissolution of an Empire*:

"When a little later, the armies of Admiral Koltchak (the White Russian Commander) took possession of Ekaterinburg, it became hideously clear that more than one person had been done to death in the underground cellar of Ipatieff's house; gradually a chain of evidence led to the discovery of that pitiful heap of ashes in the forest, and bit by bit the whole tragic story unfolded itself."

Thus the disciples of Lenin and Trotsky laid the foundation of the Communist Brotherhood of Man.

Whilst Russia was racked by murder, torture, rape and robbery and Greece was in the hands of the upstart opportunist, Venizelos, Princess Marina and her family faced exile and near-poverty in Switzerland.

Her father, Prince Nicholas, could have lived on borrowed money for quite a time. Instead, he took a little studio in the town, put up a card on the door, "Nicholas Le Prince", and made up his mind to earn his living as an artist without using the social lever of his rank and title.

Meanwhile, although he did not know it, the jewels which Bertie Stopford had smuggled out of Russia were shortly to become the property of his wife, Princess Nicholas. For her mother, the Grand Duchess Valdimir, worn out by her appalling sufferings in Russia, died at Contrexeville. Her jewellery passed to her daughter.

Even when this fortune in stones arrived, Prince Nicholas still went on with his painting, determined to live by the art he loved. He held an exhibition of his pictures at Montreux, carefully concealed his identity.

They were hailed instantly as the work of an unknown but brilliant artist. He sold the lot at good prices. Not one buyer knew his identity. After that his painting became a regular source of income.

Prince Nicholas's views on "modern art" as he expressed them in 1926, are as true today as they were then. He wrote with an almost uncanny sense of prophecy:

" 'Modern art' today goes on and on with all other modern atrocities grafted on our system by the lovers of neurotic disorder, who do not shrink from borrowing their inspirations from the dreams of lunatics

. . . Art seems rapidly to be losing the very object of its existence;
for, instead of seeking to express in form, colour, and sound all that
is beautiful, which lifts the spirit and mind to a sphere of higher
perfection, it lends itself to a degrading manifestation of coarseness
and vulgarity.

"The glorious epochs of refinement and culture, which have inspired
and given birth to the masterpieces that we continue to marvel at in
our museums and concert halls, have yielded to decadence, which in-
dulges in smeary daubs, and revels in the discordant sounds of jazz-
bands and the indecent rhythms of African dances!"

Somehow one can almost hear the twin, approving roars of applause
from the Lions of Dedham and Ampthill, my friends the late Sir Alfred
Munnings and Professor Sir Albert Richardson, who have carried the
standard for truth and decency in art which Prince Nicholas raised.

These then were the plain, uncompromising views of a man who
worshipped beauty for beauty's own sake. He learnt to paint because
he loved it. Then he painted the hard way because it had to keep him
and his family. Thus he proved himself. His constant disciple in the
studio was Marina.

Her uncle, Prince Christopher, says she was "clever and artistic
like her father. When she was a child she used to run into his studio
where the rest of the household never dared to penetrate and daub his
paints all over her fingers, in an attempt to copy him. She coaxed him
into giving her lessons in drawing and made such progress that he
arranged for her to study art seriously. When she grew older they
spent many hours sketching together."

Prince Christopher goes on to say that, one day, whilst Marina sat
by the window "drawing as usual" the family was solemnly discussing
the upheaval caused by the fact that her eldest sister Olga had suddenly
broken off her engagement to the Crown Prince Frederick of
Denmark.

The rest of the family had completely forgotten the small girl
at her sketching board when suddenly she said, with childish clarity:

"Why on earth should Olga marry him if she doesn't love him? I
wouldn't. . . ."

Her mother smiled:

"Out of the mouths of babes . . ."

Later, Olga met Prince Paul of Yugoslavia. They fell in love at first
sight. Their marriage has been ideally happy ever since.

As she grew older Princess Marina studied art seriously in Paris.

She went about the city, unaccompanied, like any other girl. She travelled on buses and on the Metro. In spite of her father's income from painting there was still little money for luxuries.

So, as her uncle, Prince Christopher, says, "she learnt things not usually included in the education of a princess . . . to make herself useful in the running of the house, to arrange flowers as well as any florist and to wear a dress from a small dressmaker so charmingly that it looked like a model from one of the *grands couturiers*. In the process she developed independence, much knowledge of life and a great understanding of human nature."

From those down-to-earth years of youth the Duchess of Kent derives her exquisite dress-sense and her "great understanding of human nature".

Her uncle adds this sidelight on her character:

"By those who do not know her ways she is sometimes misjudged for her very shyness and ultra-sensitive air of reserve create a false impression of hauteur. Underneath it she has a kindness and sympathy that one rarely encounters, an unfailing sense of humour for her own troubles and an unlimited compassion for those of other people."

Meanwhile, in Greece, more tragedy dogged the family. Her cousin, the young King Alexander, had fallen in love with Aspasie Mano, the daughter of King Constantine's A.D.C. She was exquisitely beautiful with the profile of a classic nymph. They had known each other since children.

King Alexander decided to marry her without asking the consent either of his father or of the head of the Church. So, late one November night, a priest living in a humble street in Athens, heard loud knocking at his door. He got out of bed, went downstairs and opened it.

Two men told him that his services were urgently required. They refused to tell him anything more and practically forced him into a car. He was driven to a private house. The door slammed behind him. He was taken to a lofty room. There a few people were assembled. To the priest's utter astonishment one was young King Alexander, the other the beautiful Mademoiselle Mano. He was ordered to marry them. He did so.

When the secret leaked out the usually democratic and easy-going Greeks were furious. The man-in-the-street argued furiously that for the King to marry a Greek commoner was letting the Throne down. Years before they had invited their King George I from Denmark to

come and rule because they did not want to choose a king from among
themselves!

So the wretched Mademoiselle Aspasie Mano, although recognized
legally as wife of their King, was denied the title of Queen. She was
known simply as Madame Mano—without rank or Royal privilege.
She was banished from Athens. Her husband, the King, had to remain.

Yet, when a daughter was born, the infant was given the title of
Her Royal Highness Princess Alexandra of Greece. A bitter farce.

That marriage took place in November, 1919. Less than a year later,
in October, 1920, King Alexander, alone in Greece, virtually a prisoner
in his own country, went for a walk on his estate at Tatoi. He had been
tinkering with his motor-bicycle and was wearing a chauffeur's overall. He took his favourite Alsatian dog for a walk.

On the way back to the house he called to see the vineyard keeper
and his wife who lived in a cottage near the walled garden. They had a
pair of pet monkeys. One of the monkeys bit him in the arm and leg.

The vineyard keeper's wife rushed him into the house, ripped up
the trouser-leg and dressed both wounds. She telephoned to Athens
for a surgeon to come instantly to Tatoi. He turned up two hours later
and did everything possible.

That night severe blood-poisoning set in. It was caused by bits of
the dirty overall which had been driven deep into the wound by the
monkey's teeth. Days of agony and high temperature followed. The
celebrated Doctor Vidal came from Paris. It was useless. King Alexander, that sad and gallant young man whom Fate had parted from his
wife and family, died in agony.

The upstart dictator, Venizelos, would not even allow his grandmother, Queen Olga, to visit him in his last hours. It was the crowning
sardonic tragedy.

Venizelos then offered the Throne to Prince Paul, King Constantine's third son. He refused with dignity since neither his father nor his
elder brother had renounced their rights of succession.

Then, swollen with his own importance, Venizelos decided to fight
an election with the restoration of King Constantine as the main issue.
He was convinced that he had stamped his own personality so firmly
on the country that the people would vote overwhelmingly for him
and against the King.

The result of the election was the complete defeat of Venizelos! The
people wanted their King back. Venizelos left Athens by night, slinking
away like a beaten dog.

The anti-Venizelos party elected Mr. Ralli as Prime Minister. He immediately offered the Regency of Greece to Queen Olga, Princess Marina's grandmother. Then occurred a little scene, almost comic had it not been charged with real emotion.

The aged statesman was so overcome with joy when he entered the Queen's presence that he knelt before her and kissed her hand. She begged the Prime Minister to rise. He refused. So the Queen went down on her knees opposite him, "assuring him that she would not get up unless he did".

It is surely the first time in history that a queen and a prime minister have celebrated the restoration of a throne by indulging in a kneeling match!

King Constantine then asked for a plebiscite to be taken for, or against, his return to the Throne. It took place on December 14th, 1920. The result was an overwhelming defeat for Venizelos, a resounding victory for the King. Out of 1,010,788 electors only 10,883 voted against the King's return.

The result was greeted with tears of joy in Princess Marina's home. Telegrams of congratulation overwhelmed them.

When the King and the Royal family reached Athens the whole city went mad with joy.

Prince Nicholas, who had taken his family, including Marina, back to Athens, described the arrival of the Royal train in these words:

"The Royal train had been shunted on to a side-line which, running through one of the streets, ended at a small square, where we awaited its arrival. When they saw it coming about a mile off, the people could not contain their emotion. The cry, 'Erchetai! Erchetai!' (He is coming! He is coming!)—which had been the password ever since they heard that the King was on his way to Greece—rose like the roar of an ocean wave. The engine, all beflagged, was painfully ploughing its way through a seething mass of people yelling, crying, gesticulating, sobbing hysterically. Men were hanging on to the engine and the steps of the carriage like flies. Slowly the train crawled to its destination, and came to a halt in front of where our mother stood. She stepped first into the carriage, and we followed her to greet the King. It would be impossible to describe his emotion; imagine what deep sorrows he had been through, and what this spontaneous manifestation of loyalty and love from his people meant to him!

"When the King and Queen alighted and had to walk a distance of about twenty yards to reach their carriage, they were literally assaulted.

almost crushed, by a population driven mad by uncontrollable joy. To keep order, or protect the King against any danger, was out of the question, but, then, could he be better guarded than by the people who loved him?

"As the Royal carriage slowly advanced it was all the coachman and grooms could do to control the six horses in this maddened crowd. But step by step they moved onwards, the carriage almost lifted off the ground by the people pressing against it from all sides; and so great was their desire to assure themselves that all this was not a dream, but that their Sovereign was actually again in their midst, that they hung on to the sides of the carriage and stretched out their hands to him, whilst tears streamed down their faces."

Princess Marina had just celebrated her fourteenth birthday on December 13th, the day before the plebiscite which resulted in the overwhelming victory for the King and the return of her own family to the home of her childhood. No little girl, hounded out of her own country by the impersonal, implacable forces of politics, could have received a more splendid birthday present.

She came back to the white, square and lovely house set in its great walled gardens of green lawns where the bougainvilleas and oleanders made waves of colour. Back to the blue skies of Greece, the gleam of the sea out in the bay, romps and games on the lawn; picnics once again at Tatoi although three-quarters of those beloved pine- and fir-forests had been swept and blackened by fire and the house of happy childhood memories was a burnt-out shell, but recently rebuilt.

There were old friends to be greeted almost with tears, always with laughter. Old servants who, with warm southern spontaneity, knelt at her feet, kissed her hands, wept with joy. A fairy-tale home-coming for a fairy-tale princess who had already learned through hard and bitter tragedy and murder that the world was far from being a fairy-land.

She was only fourteen but already she knew that the small cousins with whom she had played four years before in Russia; the aunts and uncles whom she had adored, had been killed like cattle.

Moreover, the years of exile in Switzerland had taught her that many so-called friends who had fawned on her parents and herself when they were Royal personages in Athens had no time for penniless Royalty living on borrowed money in a rented flat.

Those bitter experiences when Princess Marina was hardly in her teens left a lasting imprint on her character. A sense of insecurity. It accounts for her occasional air of reserve today, those transient moods of remoteness which even her closest friends cannot penetrate.

She learned in those childish years the cold fact that too many people like one for what one has in power, rank or wealth and not for what one is as a human person. That is why she values loyalty above all else in her friends today.

Whatever shadows these tragedies and disillusions may have cast on her young mind the return to her beloved home in Athens, a week after her fourteenth birthday, was the supreme joy of the moment. Soon there were picnic parties with other little girls; bathing parties in the clear, warm sea, afterwards drying in the sun on the grey, sun-kissed rocks.

There was a wedding between Princess Helen, eldest daughter of King Constantine, and King Carol of Rumania, then Crown Prince. Princess Marina was a bridesmaid at that wedding which was to turn so soon into tragic disillusionment for the bride.

Princess Marina wore a dress of Irish lace which was a complete change from her usual party frock and made the occasion enormously important in her own eyes.

One particular game which she played with her sisters and friends was that of "keeping house", in a fig-tree on an island opposite Spetsae where the Princesses spent their summer.

Baroness Helena von der Hoven writes of this forgotten idyll:

"It (the fig-tree) was called 'The House'. One crossed in a sailing boat to this island and picnicked on the beach. Then one climbed the tree. Each member of the party had her own branch which represented her 'room' and all the figs on this branch were entirely her property. One could visit each other and exchange fruit which was carefully passed over on fresh green leaves. It needed a lot of agility not to drop any and if such a misfortune happened it was greeted with a lot of merry laughter and jokes.

"Though one of the youngest, Princess Marina was always the ring-leader and kept the company in fits of laughter by mimicking her governess of whom she gave striking imitations. There were also other pranks which necessitated a certain amount of tactics and daring, and her contemporaries learnt to know so well that humorous, half-wistful, half-mischievous smile of young Princess Marina.

"One of the favourite games in those days was shooting arrows. The bows were home-made out of flexible branches tied firmly with a bit of string and great competition took place as to who should produce the best weapon. It was great fun hiding behind trees and rocks and shooting at invisible enemies, and Robin Hood and other similar heroes were very popular at that time."

All this was short-lived. The home-coming turned to ashes all too soon. Within two years King Constantine lost his throne for good and Princess Marina's family were hounded again into exile.

King Constantine had inherited a hornets' nest of trouble. Venizelos had left the King the legacy of a war in Asia Minor against the New Turkey of Mustapha Kemal. Lloyd George and Venizelos had hatched the Asia Minor campaign. Lloyd George saw in it a first-class chance to use Greece as a cat's-paw to further British interests in the Near East without spilling one drop of British blood.

Venizelos saw in it a rosy vision of a Greater Greece beyond the Aegean Sea with Turkey finally humbled to the dust and all Greece kneeling before him as the Great Empire Builder. The only thing he forgot was the fact that the Greek Army was not strong enough to do the job unaided. Under the Treaty of Sèvres he had committed Greece to this adventure.

King Constantine wanted peace with Turkey. On the other hand he could not withdraw the Greek Armies from Asia Minor without exposing the flourishing Greek population in those parts to the vengeance of the Turks whose anger had been brought to flaming point by Venizelos's policy.

The Greek Government decided on general mobilization with the idea of winning the war quickly.

They put more than 310,000 men into the field.

Whilst these men were fighting in the heart of Asia Minor, Venizelist agents did everything to undermine the morale of the Army and that of the population at home. They even wrote pamphlets which Mustapha Kemal dropped from planes into the Greek trenches telling the serving men of the sufferings of their families at home and accusing the King of continuing the war in order to consolidate himself on the Throne. General Harington, who was at Constantinople at the time, knew of all this.

King Constantine led his own troops in the field. Princess Marina's father and her Uncle Andrew, father of the present Duke of Edinburgh, accompanied the King and Crown Prince and fought in the field.

The Greek Army started off with lightning success. They drove the Turks back hundreds of kilometres until Kemal was fighting with his back to the wall. Then was the time for a treaty with Turkey and an

Portrait by Cecil Beaton

Visit to Yugoslavia: the Duke and Duchess of Kent at Bled with Prince Paul, the Duchess's brother-in-law

Preparing for the Coronation of King George VI. The Duke and Duchess of Kent leaving Westminster Abbey accompanied by the Duke of Norfolk (left) and followed by Lord and Lady Louis Mountbatten

end of the war, for the Greeks had overrun their resources, their lines of communication and their strength.

Colonel A'Court Repington, the famous British military correspondent and tactical expert, lunched with Princess Marina's father one day at the height of the crisis. He said:

"Believe me, your only way out of the difficulties is to ignore the Powers and come to a direct understanding with Kemal."

Prince Nicholas adds:

"Alas, the advice could not be followed for fear of serious misunderstanding with England."

Finally, Greece decided to leave the decision to the Powers. Lloyd George then announced that until a Conference could be called the Greek Army had *to remain where it was and repulse all attacks of the Turks, otherwise any further discussion was useless.*

He offered neither money nor troops. Greece was left to hold the bag.

Winter came on. The Greek soldiers had to face a temperature of twenty-five degrees below zero. Ill-clad, ill-fed, they suffered bitterly whilst the much-delayed Conference was put off and put off. Meanwhile, Kemal artfully played for time whilst he built up his army and fighting resources. The Powers merely talked and told the Greeks to stay where they were and shiver in the snow.

On August 26th, 1922, Kemal fell upon the Greek Army like the Hammer of Thor. The Greeks put up a heroic resistance for two days. Then they broke. Defeat degenerated into disorder and disorder into panic. Many troops were lost in the mountains. Others died fighting. Thousands surrendered. The Turks not only smashed the Greek Army but they sacked the city of Smyrna and butchered thousands of the wretched Christian population with sadistic cruelty.

Luckily, Princess Marina had been sent to England with "dear Foxy" whilst her mother was in Paris with her two elder sisters. At first she stayed at a hotel in Kensington and then she moved to Warlingham in Surrey. She visited Queen Mary at Windsor Castle and her great-aunt, Queen Alexandra, whom she resembled in many ways, at Sandringham. Both worshipped her. They had written many affectionate letters and sent presents at Christmas to her and her sisters whilst they were in exile in Switzerland.

Meanwhile, in Greece, the thunder broke. Mutiny swept the Army. The King was the scapegoat. The Venizelists saw to that. All disasters were blamed on him. The pro-German slander was revived. Army officers demanded his abdication at sword-point in favour of his son, Prince George.

So, on October 30th, 1922, less than two years after he had returned to Athens to the boom of cannon, the ringing of bells, and tears of joy, King Constantine left Greece forever. His old soldiers at Tatoi sobbed like children. Groups of peasants, merchants, society people, shepherds and their wives saw him off in tears.

Admiral Aubrey Smith, head of the British Naval Mission, arranged the last sad exit with infinite courtesy and understanding. Princess Marina's father put the final moments into poignant prose:

"It was dark when the steamer started—the wind was howling. One by one the lights of the little village as we sailed away, faded into the distance. This was the last time King Constantine gazed on his beloved Greece."

It broke his heart. He died three months later at Palermo.

Prince Nicholas, who left Greece with the King, cabled to his wife and two elder daughters in Paris and to Princess Marina in England asking them to join him at once in Palermo.

There the little family re-united. Once more their roots had been torn up. Their old home had gone for good. Their fortune was confiscated. A Republic ruled in Greece. For the second time they were wanderers on the face of the earth.

Princess Marina, then a tall, delicately formed sixteen-year-old, slender as a fawn, looked at her parents and said, with that sudden touch of mischief which lit her face sometimes in the darkest hours:

"We really needn't have unpacked our trunks."

CHAPTER SIX

Second Exile, Poverty, the Firing Squad—and Smuggled Jewels

WHEN THE TRAIN pulled into Paris with Princess Marina and her family on board they took a taxi. On other visits a magnificent limousine had been ordered and waiting. A luxurious hotel. Parties. Shopping in the best shops. Punch and Judy shows. Marvellous cakes. Mouth-watering sweets for small girls. And a constant stream of callers at the hotel, princes, princesses, the French nobility, international millionaires, statesmen, politicians—the cream of Society.

This time a little middle-class hotel near the Bois de Boulogne. Stuffy, cramped rooms, indifferent meals and, instead of the cream of Society, the sour milk of neglect. Exiled royalties without money were not particularly popular, especially when it looked as though they were exiled for good.

That was the bleak picture of disillusion. Even the children, in their early, impressionable teens, noticed the cold indifference of many former so-called friends.

Prince and Princess Nicholas faced that arid future with dignity and determination. He took a studio at Auteuil, painted all day and sold his pictures at good prices. She, born the Grand Duchess Helen of Russia, set her heart and hands to help the thousands of Russian refugees who, escaping murder by the skin of their teeth, had flocked to Paris. The cost of living in Paris then was lowest of any capital city in Europe. It was not low enough to prevent many Russian children and their parents from reaching the border of starvation.

Princess Marina went every Sunday with her mother and sisters to the Russian Orthodox Church. There they met Russian princesses, grand duchesses, land-owners, merchants, working men, cab-drivers, waiters, seamstresses and others—all in the same boat. Few or none had money. Most had lost fathers, mothers, children or sweethearts, murdered, imprisoned or just vanished into the cold blackness of oblivion.

Princes and generals drove taxi-cabs. Princesses worked as waitresses,

67

mannequins, midinettes or plain servants. Men who had owned thousands of acres of forest and farms were doorkeepers. Through every class of society ran the tale of disillusionment, despair and drudgery.

It was worst for the children. Uprooted from their native Russia, often crowded with their parents in single rooms, ill-clad, toyless, half-starved, they were utterly pathetic.

Princess Nicholas decided that, as she could do nothing for Greece owing to the political upheaval, she would give her spare time, energy and resources to help these wretched, stranded Russians.

The jewels that Bertie Stopford had smuggled out of Russia came to her when her mother, the Grand Duchess Vladimir, died as a result of the frightful privations she had suffered in Russia and during her escape from it.

Those jewels were worth a fortune. They could have transported Prince Nicholas and his family from a middle-class hotel near the Bois to the Ritz or the George Cinq. They could have meant ease, luxury and no worry.

Princess Nicholas put the facts squarely to her husband and her daughters. She considered that she held the jewels in trust for the children. Would they, and her husband, agree to her selling some of them and using the proceeds to set up a home and school for destitute Russian children of all parties? They agreed instantly.

Princess Nicholas and her daughters threw themselves into the work. They organized dances, charity shows, sales, fêtes and anything else to raise money. Princess Marina sold programmes, gathered in subscriptions, helped her mother with hundreds of letters, whipped up enthusiasm and help. No one could resist the slim, fair, elegant girl in her teens with the amber eyes and half-mischievous smile, the embodiment of youth and freshness. They not only got the home going but they kept it going. A young Englishwoman came forward with generous financial help. Her name was Dorothy Paget, daughter of Lord Queensborough—one of the most famous women racehorse owners in Britain.

Princess Marina made a revealing remark to an old family friend, Baroness von der Hoven, about that time. She had spent days trying to raise money from all sorts of people for the children's home.

"It is the poor who help the most," she said. "Especially the English people. They are so kind. Once you have gained their friendship they never let you down."

That was the spontaneous tribute of a seventeen-year-old girl who had known all too much of human misery and ingratitude. She did not dream that one day England would be her home.

Meanwhile, in Greece tragedy walked starkly. When King Constantine was hounded out of the country by Venizelos, his elder son, Prince George, was put on a lonely throne as a puppet king. George II of Greece was virtually a prisoner in his own palace. That state of affairs lasted only a short while. Soon he was deposed and a Republic set up.

During this period, Prince Andrew of Greece, father of the Duke of Edinburgh, then a mere small boy, had been recalled from his home in Corfu to Athens by the Venizelos Government to give evidence at the trial of five Greek Ministers, utterly loyal members of King Constantine's former government.

They were now accused of having instigated the disastrous war in Asia Minor which had led to the ultimate defeat of Greece, the hideous massacre of thousands of the inhabitants of Smyrna by the Turks and the banishment of King Constantine as chief scapegoat.

That campaign, as I remarked earlier, had been planned by Lloyd George and Venizelos against the King's wish and judgement.

Now the five Ministers, Gounaris, Stratos, Protopapadakis, Baltazzis, Théotokis and General Hadjanesti, the Commander-in-Chief of the Army, were on trial for their lives.

When Prince Andrew, who had commanded an army corps, arrived at Athens to give evidence, as he thought, on behalf of these six men, he was clapped under close arrest. He was charged with military incompetence.

Venizelos was controlling the country from outside—like a ghastly spider lurking in a dark corner on the edge of his web. His puppet, General Pangalos, who had been at school with Prince Andrew, was Minister of War and Military Dictator. He carried out Venizelos's orders.

Those orders included the enticement of Prince Andrew to Athens, his immediate arrest, his execution as quickly as possible.

No one was allowed near the Prince except his valet. When he broke a tooth and suffered agony in his jaw, he was denied a dentist. All letters were opened. All parcels confiscated. All food sent in by friends was cut open. When one dear old lady sent him a jar of *foie gras* in aspic, it was chopped to pieces before he was allowed to eat it.

His brother, Prince Christopher of Greece, Princess Marina's other uncle, a brave man, a great musician, a soldier and a wit, arrived in Athens on a passport which allowed him to stay only eight days. He tried to get a message to Prince Andrew in prison. It was forbidden. So he wrote a letter on thin rice paper, rolled it in a cigarette, put the cigarette among others in the cigarette-case of Prince Andrew's valet. Thus the brothers communicated.

Back came a short note. Prince Andrew that morning had been interviewed by General Pangalos, his former school-mate.

"How many children have you?" Pangalos snapped suddenly. Prince Andrew told him.

"Poor little things! What a pity they'll be orphans so soon," Pangalos answered.

Little did the young Duke of Edinburgh-to-be know that, at that moment, his father's fate hung in the balance by a matter of hours.

Meanwhile, King George V of England; King Alfonso of Spain and Monsieur Poincaré, President of France, sent urgent protests to Venizelos to stop the executions. Princess Marina's grandmother had implored all three to do their utmost to save Andrew's life.

A personal friend of my own, the late Sir Gerald Talbot, was at that moment on his way from London to Athens as the special envoy of King George V. The Pope, too, had despatched his Legate. Even Venizelos could not ignore such powerful protests.

That night, however, he sent a telegram to Pangalos.

"Whatever you have to do, do it quickly. Tomorrow may be too late."

The next morning, in the cold dawn, the five Ministers and General Hadjanesti, were hustled out of their cells into the prison courtyard. They were lined up against the wall. A file of soldiers facing them raised their rifles. At the command, they fired. The six men dropped, writhing in their last agonies. No time even for a prayer before they went to their God.

Such was the utter blood-lust of Venizelos, the opportunist whose ambition wrecked the throne of Greece, drove her Army to defeat, caused massacres, mass arrests, assassinations and this crowning legal farce of plain murder.

A few hours later Gerald Talbot arrived in Athens. Too late to save the Ministers and the General. Just in time to save Prince Andrew.

Somewhere a little fair-haired boy named Philip was wandering in the garden of a sunny villa in Corfu, called Mon Repos, wondering what had happened to his daddy.

Hard on the heels of Talbot came the King of Spain's A.D.C. Then the Papal Legate with a protest from the Pope. Too late again. The six dead men were in their coffins.

Prince Christopher was in Athens during that week of death and drama. His lawyer, Mr. Caralou, whose wife had been his governess and afterwards lady-in-waiting to his mother, warned him to get out instantly. So, with the help of his lawyer and Mr. Stucker, his old tutor, he collected his bonds and securities and packed all the jewellery belonging to Princess Marina's mother in a wooden box. He also collected Prince Nicholas's money and securities—and a large white Persian cat. With it Princess Marina had played many times. It was her mother's dearest pet.

That cat nearly lost everything.

Tiaras, brooches, bracelets, rings, necklaces, parures and ropes of pearls were packed in a rough wooden box so shaky that its bottom was almost falling out. Not the sort of box you would suspect of conveying a fortune. They forgot the cat!

Prince Christopher arranged to leave on an Italian steamer as secretly as possible. He drove down to the quay with Mr. Stucker and Mr. Caralou in his oldest clothes. They crammed themselves into a little rowing boat, hardly large enough to hold three men, two large suitcases, a rickety wooden box and a wicker basket—with disgruntled cat.

He wrote, of that tense moment: "It was nerve-racking, for until we got clear of the landing stage, I fully expected some of the harbour officials would recognize us and detain me. Fortunately their attention was concentrated on the public launch which was just then disembarking passengers from the steamer and our little craft passed unnoticed."

Not, however, by everyone. As Prince Christopher sat down in the boat, the cat, no sailor, started to yowl. It spat. It scratched. It yelled. Its miaows ascended in protest to the Athenian skies.

And at least a score of interested Athenians on the quay turned and stared hard at the hunched and shabbily dressed man with the air of distinction, who sat cuddling a wicker basket, packed with furred protest. Any one of those passengers could have recognized him. For the Royal family of Greece had always moved among the people as freely as the next man.

Prince Christopher thumped the basket to make the cat shut up. It yelled more piercingly.

At that moment one suitcase burst open. Stocks, share certificates and money spilled out. Mr. Stucker stuffed them back, red-faced, praying that no guard would see them.

Then they rowed off to the Italian steamer. The gangway was down. At the top stood a Greek sentry, armed, with orders to examine every passport! Venizelos was taking no chances of Prince Christopher or any other member of Princess Marina's family escaping by that ship. Prince "Cristo" took one look at the sentry.

"They were going to detain me at the last moment," he wrote afterwards, "so I ran full speed up the gangway. Instead of stopping when the sentry barred my way I delivered him a tremendous blow in the stomach which doubled him up. Then, before he could recover, I sprang past him and rushed into my cabin."

Once there the Prince was safe. He was on Italian ground and the Greek sentry had no power to arrest him. That petrified soldier was still gasping, and holding his solar plexus, when Mr. Stucker pushed past him on board with all the luggage. He did not even examine Stucker's passport.

Thus, the modest fortune and family jewels of Princess Marina's parents were smuggled out of Greece when death ruled Athens.

The sentry was finished—but not the cat. That night the boat called at Brindisi. The Prince went ashore with the luggage, the jewels and the cat. He took a room at an hotel.

Next morning, a quarter of an hour before he was due to catch his train to Palermo he lifted the lid of the basket. Out shot the cat. It scratched him, whisked out of the door, streaked down the corridor and shot into a bedroom. In bed was an elderly English spinster. She loathed cats! Her shrieks ruined a dozen breakfasts. A waiter dived under the bed, bagged the cat, crammed it in the basket and slammed the lid down.

Prince Christopher fled downstairs clutching cat and jewels, jumped into a waiting car and drove to the station at break-neck speed. He rushed down the platform, followed by Stucker, panting, with suitcases and hurled himself into the train with one minute to spare.

Royal arrivals in Greece were usually occasions of drama. This exit was no less.

There was no sleeper on the train but the Prince and Stucker had a compartment to themselves. They stretched themselves out on the seats and tried to sleep. But not the cat. "It yelled so heartrendingly," wrote Prince "Cristo", "that people passing along the corridor cast glances of indignation in our direction."

When they reached Palermo the cat escaped again. It got under the seat. It hid behind the hot-water pipes. Neither floor nor pipes had been swept for ages. It refused to move. So a porter grabbed it by the tail and hauled it out. The white and royal Persian was now a spitting fury covered in soot.

When Prince Christopher arrived at the Hotel Villa Igea where King Constantine was staying with some of his family, Princess Helen gave one scream when she saw the cat.

"Cristo! What *have* you done to the poor thing?" she cried indignantly.

"What hasn't it done to *me*," he retorted. "That's no ordinary cat. I believe it's a devil!"

Princess Helen took her cat, soothed it, brushed it, petted it, talked to it. Then she took it out to the terrace for a little sun and peace. There, licking its paws, sat Queen Sophie's grey mongrel cat. This aged pet had so far lived the decorous life usually accorded to a retired lady-in-waiting.

Prince Christopher was in his bath—relaxing, ". . . when I heard a pandemonium of snarls, shrieks and hisses on the terrace."

He sprang out of the bath, looked out of the window huddling a towel round his shoulders. There below, in the midst of a circle of scandalized Royalties, he saw, "two infuriated balls, one a dirty white, the other grey, whirling in the midst of a cloud of dust and flying fur.

"My brother Nicholas was running round them trying to separate them with a tiny jug of water taken from his breakfast tray. . . . A nun from the Convent of Blue Sisters, with veil and robes flying, rushed into the fray with a sunshade snatched up from a chair.

"Finally my brother with a well-directed kick, sent them hurtling through the air, one into a rose-bush, the other into an orange tree, where they stayed for hours licking their wounds."

The cat-fight was the one shaft of comic relief in those grey days.

The Italians were kindness itself to King Constantine and his family. The King had aged years in a few months. He could still laugh at the whirling cats and the doubled-up sentry but "he was like a ghost among the living. His heart was broken," said Prince Christopher.

"When I left by boat he came down to the landing stage with us. I looked back and saw the tall soldierly figure standing there in the light of the setting sun waving to us. Suddenly a mist rose in front of my eyes. I had a premonition that I was never going to see my brother again." King Constantine died within three months.

The King who had twice thrashed the Turkish Army and put them on the run, the King who was adored by his soldiers, foresters, shepherds and everyday people, yet was twice exiled by the satanic plotting of Venizelos, died because life held no more.

Meanwhile, in Athens, Prince Andrew's farcical trial drew to a close. But for the arrival of Gerald Talbot with the letter from King George V, followed by the Spanish King's A.D.C. and the Papal Legate, he would, days before, have been a bullet-riddled corpse.

In Corfu, Princess Alice, his wife, daughter of Prince Louis of Battenberg, waited, ashen-faced, for news. In Paris, Princess Marina's grandmother and her Aunt Minnie waited in their suite at the Ritz, besieged by reporters, racked by suspense.

The trial ended on a Saturday. They sat up all night waiting for news. None came. Early in the morning Princess Marina's grandmother, haggard, wan with worry, went to the Russian Church to pray.

Prince Christopher waited by the telephone. At ten o'clock it rang. He picked up the receiver, his hand shaking. A voice said:

"This is the *New York Herald* speaking. Your brother is to be exiled, not shot."

He leapt downstairs, jumped into a car with his sister and drove at top speed to the church. Queen Olga was just coming out.

When she saw them she went deathly white. Her hand flew to her heart.

"He's safe! He's safe! It's all right," they cried.

Whilst kings and a dictator played pitch-and-toss with her uncle Andrew's life, Princess Marina was still in the schoolroom in Paris.

She learnt languages quickly, read Jane Austen and Mary Webb and most of Balzac. She adored music and started serious portrait painting. In Switzerland, during their first exile, she had sketched landscapes and added little figures to them. Now, in Paris, she really began to paint people, and to take art seriously.

She often walked with her mother from the hotel to Prince Nicholas's studio to fetch him back to lunch. Otherwise he would forget that it was time to eat and go on painting. Even at that age she discussed and criticized his work with the candour of a fellow artist and not just as a daughter.

"Marina's praise always pleases me," Prince Nicholas said. "She never praises something which she doesn't like and does not consider good."

She had already developed good taste in clothes, particularly hats. "Marina *does* something to a hat," her father once remarked. "She can put on any hat and look just right in it."

She often adjusted a hat or a scarf on her mother or sisters because her artistic eye could not bear something that was not precisely right. The wrong colour or wrong shape of a dress really irritated her.

She could mimic anyone—an actress, a singer, a friend, an eccentric or a pomposity. But it was kindly mimicking. She never willingly hurt anyone. Baroness von der Hoven, who saw a lot of her during those formative years, says:

"She never took anything for granted and I often heard her say how kind people were if they rendered her the slightest service. In fact, her whole attitude to life was extremely modest."

Another endearing quality was the fact that she seldom looked for her pleasures outside the family circle. She was happiest with her parents and sisters, whether it was a visit to the theatre; the ballet, which she adores; a sketching expedition; a visit to an art gallery—she and her father must have visited every good gallery in Paris; a dance, or merely shopping. Whatever it was she wanted her family with her.

She had little money to spend on clothes, but she was always well-dressed. She was *chic* in the city which invented the word. She could make her own clothes and alter things to perfection. She always had original ideas for making almost any dress look excitingly different without being *outré*.

She and her father often went sketching in the Paris streets, on the river bank and in the country.

One day they were painting near the cemetery at Passy. A little girl and her mother stopped and stared. The small child pointed to Prince Nicholas and Princess Marina, both busy with their paint boxes.

"Are those musicians, Mummy?" she asked. "Do we have to give them a sou?"

The most amusing episode of all happened when Prince Nicholas was sketching by himself on the Seine embankment. A stevedore off a river boat, in coal-blackened dungarees, blue shirt and beret, strolled up, studied his painting, pointed to it and said:

"I suppose this costs millions of francs."

"No, I wouldn't say millions," Prince Nicholas said quietly, "I don't expect to get more than a few hundred francs for it."

"*Tiens!*" said the stevedore, cogitating deeply. "They say there's a Dutchman called Rubens who paints pictures and they're worth millions."

"Ah, that's quite another matter," Prince Nicholas answered. "You see, Rubens is a Great Master and his pictures are worth millions."

"Have you ever met him?" the stevedore said eagerly.

"No. I've never had the pleasure of meeting Rubens," the Prince answered. "You see, he died just a few hundred years before I was born."

The stevedore shut up and walked off. He felt he had put his foot in it.

When Prince Nicholas went home to tea and told the family of this conversation, Princess Marina exclaimed:

"How *could* you have been so cruel to that poor river man? I'd have told him that, of course, I knew Rubens very well as he was a great man and I would have left that poor stevedore quite happy with his illusions and the pleasant feeling that he, too, knew something about art."

"You know, I think Marina was absolutely right. She had the human angle," Prince Nicholas said to Baroness von der Hoven afterwards.

When her eldest sister, Princess Olga, married Prince Paul of Yugoslavia, Princess Marina went for a year as a boarder, from the age of sixteen to seventeen, to a finishing school run by Princess Mestchersky who was an old friend of the family. She had opened the school for girls of all nationalities in order to earn a living for herself and to do something useful at the same time.

Princess Marina was homesick at first but she soon took to boardingschool life, made lots of friends and thoroughly enjoyed herself. She studied the French language, French History and Literature, elocution and essay writing, for which she had a particular flair.

She also attended special art classes under Madame Valentin, an extremely cultured, well-read woman. She was not only an authority on China, Chinese art and politics as well as being an expert art teacher, but she gave her pupils up-to-date commentaries on such things as the economic state of America and the industrial development of England.

With Madame Valentin, Princess Marina and the other girls visited Fontainebleau, Versailles and other lovely and historic places around Paris. One spring, she and the other schoolgirls went by motor-coach to see the famous chateaux on the River Loire. They spent two heavenly days touring that enchanted valley when the lilac bushes were in bloom in old, forgotten gardens and nightingales sang in the river stillness at dusk.

The other girls voted her "a good sport" and she made a lot of friends. She was allowed to go home every Sunday afternoon and evening after church in the morning and her parents and her sister Elizabeth often visited her during term-time.

She had a tiny bedroom to herself at school, furnished in pink chintz with a few photographs of her family and one or two of her own sketches and always, some fresh flowers.

She had a taste for intellectual games and was particularly good at anything which involved geography. Maps and the globe fascinated her.

During the holidays she often went with her mother and sister to mannequin parades. When they got home afterwards she usually put on a few dresses, one after the other, and imitated the mannequins and the various creations they had just seen.

This started the stupid rumour that she was going to be a mannequin. She was never anything of the sort. Indeed, at no time, did she ever earn her living in any form. Had she been born in other circumstances she would probably have taken up dancing and acting with painting as a second string to her bow.

The school routine was simple. Prayers at 8 a.m. Breakfast at 8.30 a.m. Princess Marina always had an English breakfast although she has never been a big eater. From 9 till 10 a.m. the girls walked to the Bois de Boulogne and back for exercise and fresh air. Lessons began sharp at 10 a.m. and ended at half-past twelve. Half an hour's break and then luncheon at 1 p.m.

The afternoon was spent visiting places of interest in Paris and they were back promptly for tea at 4.30 p.m.

Princess Marina and the other girls travelled each afternoon in Tubes and buses, so she learnt her way about Paris just like any other citizen.

After tea came lectures on various subjects, then prep., and dinner at 7.30 p.m. Then the girls were taken to see good plays or concerts by good artists. This gave her an all-round education not only in academic subjects, but in art, the theatre and everyday values.

During these years the family moved from the hotel into a smallish flat near the Avenue Henri Martin. The various cousins who had been scattered by exile, all joined up again. Prince Andrew, after he escaped from Greece with his life, settled at St. Cloud with his family. This meant that Princess Marina now had a wide circle of friends—her own cousins, as well as the writers, artists, musicians, Russian and otherwise, who frequently dropped in at the flat to talk about the theatre, painting, music and often stayed to share the simple family meals.

Meanwhile the home for refugee Russian children which her mother had started, and largely financed, at St. Germain, had grown tremendously. More than sixty boys and girls of all classes from two to twelve years old, were being cared for. Princess Marina spent many days at the home.

"She always had a way with children and seemed to understand them instinctively," one of the helpers at the home said. "She could coax the nerviest, shyest child into peace in a few minutes. It was just the way she had with them."

During these years, Princess Marina travelled quite a lot. She went over to England with her father and mother during the summer holidays of 1924 to see her sister Olga, who was expecting her first baby at White Lodge, in Richmond Park. The house had been lent to the young couple by Queen Mary and King George V. In those days England was a positive haven of rest and friendship for the exiled Royal family of Greece.

She got to know London fairly well in those days. She and her father, devoted to pictures and works of art, visited all the big art galleries and museums. They explored Soho and the City. She went shopping in the big London stores with her mother. She travelled on the Underground or went by bus with her sister. She learnt to know and love the everyday English people, their calm courtesy, their instinctive warmth of heart, hidden under the slightly stand-offish English manner. The ties with England struck their roots early.

CHAPTER SEVEN

"I Shall Never Marry Except for Love"

THE TENTH of January, 1934 was, in a sense, a turning point in Princess Marina's life. On that day her tall, dark and lovely sister, Princess Elizabeth, married Count Toerring-Jettenbach in the private chapel of Seefeld Castle near Munich.

A white and simple wedding with half the Royalty of Europe, reigning and de-throned, to wish the bride happiness. Princess Marina was happy and delighted that her sister had married the man she loved but was also, perhaps, a little wistful for herself.

Both her sisters were now married. She herself, now twenty-seven, was the only one left.

Her grandmother had married at sixteen, her mother at eighteen. She showed no signs of wanting to marry anyone.

"I shall never marry any man unless I love him," she often said. She stuck to it. The man had yet to appear. Plenty of wealthy, well-born young bachelors would gladly have married her. The ex-Crown Prince of Germany had rounded up all the eligible young men he could think of when she paid a visit to Potsdam. Her sister and brother-in-law, Prince and Princess Paul of Yugoslavia, had filled their holiday chalet at Bohinj in the Julian Alps, with agreeable young men. Princess Marina preferred picnics and boating with her girl cousins.

Four of her cousins, Prince Andrew's daughters, part of that jolly crowd who used to romp together in the woods at Tatoi and on the lawns of the white and sunny villa in Athens, had all married three years before. Their young brother, Philip, now Duke of Edinburgh, was down for school at Cheam. His father, embittered by his experiences in Greece, had decided that an English school, English values and the English way of life were best for his son.

As for his sisters, Princess Cecile was now the wife of the Hereditary Prince of Hesse-Darmstadt, Princess Theodora married the Landgraf of Baden, Princess Margarita is the wife of the Hereditary Prince of Hohenlohe Langenburg, and Princess Sophie, whom the family called "Tiny" had married Prince Christof of Hesse.

A friend, who was at the wedding at Seefeld, said afterwards:

"The starry look in her sister's eyes stirred something deep and, so far, unknown in Marina. From a lively, carefree girl she seemed to have suddenly grown into wistful womanhood. Her face acquired a new spiritual expression. She read more, she thought, perhaps she dreamt. This period of sudden spiritual growth was a vital one in her young life, and she herself must have been aware of it.

"I suddenly understood the change which had struck me in Princess Marina. I understood that the girl who was looking at me so seriously, with those golden-brown eyes, was a dreamer and a thinker. She was also an idealist; and she was hoping for these ideals and dreams to come true. I felt that she was capable of great feeling, and that the decisive moment had come for her. She would either be ideally happy or terribly hurt, and I prayed it might be the first."

About this time her eldest sister, Princess Olga, who had married Prince Paul of Yugoslavia, began to think seriously of the marital future of her youngest sister. She remembered that on previous visits to London Marina had dined and danced with a good many young men. She had talked of most of them quite freely. But not about Prince George, youngest son of King George V of England.

Soon after the second sister, Princess Elizabeth, married her dashing young Bavarian, Count Toerring-Jettenbach, Princess Olga made a sudden decision. Her young son had to go back to his English school. She and her husband would stay at Claridge's. She asked Marina to go with them.

The afternoon after they arrived at Claridge's, Princess Olga took her small son and her younger sister shopping. Prince Paul of Yugoslavia was settling down to a book in the sitting-room of their suite when young Prince George of England was announced. The two men had a lot to talk about.

When, at last, Princess Olga returned with her schoolboy son, Princess Marina was not with her. She had gone to the hairdressers. Prince George stayed on. They had tea. Prince George still stayed on. Eventually, Princess Marina arrived. Prince George stayed a little longer. He was in no hurry to go.

Princess Olga put two and two together. She had married for love herself. Moreover, she knew her younger sister's sense of values.

Thereafter, the courtship, if that is the word for a sensitive, youthful attraction of minds and interests, followed the most human lines. There was nothing about it of stiff precedent or royal protocol. They

Grandfather, father and son. Prince Nicholas watches the Duke of Kent holding
his first child, Prince Edward (the present Duke of Kent) (photograph by
Dorothy Wilding)

(*Above*) Princess Nicholas and her three daughters in Athens, 1938—a picture recalling the first photograph in this book

(*Left*) Driving to Ascot, 1938. Princess Marina's sense of style and taste quickly earned her the distinction of being one of the best dressed women in England

went to cinemas together. They motored into the country. They walked in Green Park. They laughed at the same things. They both loved pictures, good furniture, music, dancing. They met whenever they wanted.

No dynastic plans, no high principles of State, were at stake. The throne of Greece was not even in the balance any longer. The throne of England, that symbol of stability, had yet to undergo its own unforeseen convulsions. The way was clear for two young people to know each other, talk freely, understand each other, enjoy the same interests.

Prince George was then thirty-one—slim, athletic, with a clear skin, intelligent eyes, a generous smile and a quick sense of humour. As a small boy his tutors said that he could grasp almost any subject quickly, providing he was interested in it. His father, King George V, gruff, downright, bearded and benevolent, a man who could never tolerate fools lightly, said that his youngest son "had the brains of the family".

From his mother, Queen Mary, he inherited his love of pictures, fine furniture, works of art and a superb decorative sense. Had he not been a Royal prince he would have made a career as an interior decorator. Yet he was no carpet-knight, no drawing-room blossom.

He loved dancing, films and jazz, but, equally, he could ride a horse, cross a stiff hunting country, shoot and take any risks that offered.

As a young man, the story goes, he climbed Big Ben, swarming up the scaffolding from the ground, outside the House of Commons one night until he reached the dizzy topmost face of the clock.

He went to school as a boy at St. Peter's Court in the Isle of Thanet and when the raids began and bombs fell he sneaked upstairs from the cellars where the boys had been ordered to hide, to watch the bombs fall.

"Well, anyway, I can say I've seen more of the war than Harry," he remarked. Harry, his brother, the Duke of Gloucester, was then at Eton.

In those boyish days he loved wearing a kilt and wanted to go into a Highland regiment. He also loved toy boats, particularly a lugger made for him by a Deal fisherman. So the Navy it had to be, since his father, King George V, had been a sailor.

His naval career began as a cadet at Osborne in 1916. He passed out at Dartmouth in April, 1920, and by January, 1921 was a midshipman in *Iron Duke*, the flagship of the Mediterranean. He served later in *Queen Elizabeth* and the flotilla leader, *Mackay*. Then in *Hawkins*, flag-

6

ship in China; *Nelson*, flagship of the Home Fleet, and saw service on
the South African, Atlantic and West Indies stations. In the Navy he
was known as "George" or "P.G.".

As a midshipman he lived on his pay—five shillings a day or so.
King George V, always a little of a family tyrant, refused to give him
any more until he was twenty-one.

A senior naval officer who was deputed to act as "bear leader" to
the young Prince has told me the story.

"It was very difficult," he said. " 'P.G.' never had enough money
to keep up his position. Whereas you and I would tip, say, half a crown,
he was always expected to tip five shillings—a full day's pay.

"The Prince of Wales was devoted to his young brother, however,
so came to the rescue more than once!—always anxious to help.

"One day he said to me, 'What's particularly needed?'

" 'A motor-car, sir,' I answered.

"A few days later we had a message to be at York House at 5 p.m.
The Prince of Wales was there. So was a brand-new Wolseley two-
seater. His gift to his brother.

" 'Now don't forget you have to drive it in very carefully,' he said
to 'P.G.'

"We got in, drove to 'The Hut Hotel' at Ripley, had dinner and
then went on to Balmer Lawn in the New Forest. I don't think 'P.G.'
drove at more than thirty-five to forty all the way.

"Next morning we set off early to play golf at Lyndhurst. Three
miles out the most ungodly noise broke out under the bonnet. We
stopped—the car was shaking and rattling like a tin shed in a gale.

"A lorry stopped. 'Are you all right, mate?' the driver said to
Prince George.

" 'Far from it,' he answered, 'perhaps you could tell me what's
wrong.'

" 'Big-end's gone,' said the lorry-driver, after he'd had a look.

" 'Gone? Gone where? Where's it gone?' 'P.G.' said in astonishment.
I don't think he knew what a big-end was in those days. The lorry-
driver looked at him as though he was mad!

"However, they towed us back to Balmer Lawn and next day
Wolseley's sent a bigger and better car.

"Soon after he had to go into Sister Agnes's nursing home. There
he had his two little toes amputated as they were hammer toes. This
got into the newspapers.

"One morning I opened the post and among the fan-mail was a

letter from an adoring old lady. She wrote: 'I'm so sorry about your poor little toes. Why don't you have them made into a pair of earrings for your dear sister as a wedding present?'

"His sister, Princess Mary, was just about to marry Lord Lascelles. 'P.G.' thought it was a hell of a good joke.

"He had a near squeak from death whilst I was with him. The battleship *Queen Elizabeth* had a drifter attached to her called *Blue Sky*. Midshipmen went off in her to improve their seamanship. 'P.G.' begged to be allowed to go. The Captain refused. Instead, two middies, called Dundas and Cator, went in his place.

"The drifter ran into terrible weather, foundered and sank with the loss of all hands. Dundas and Cator included.

" 'P.G.' took this terribly to heart. He was so frightfully upset that Louis Greig suggested to the King that he should be posted to another ship—as he was obviously haunted by the thought of the two boys who had been drowned.

"So he was sent to *Mackay*, a destroyer flotilla leader commanded by Captain Dashwood F. Moir. I went with him. We had a wonderful cruise to the Baltic. First, Oslo, where Queen Maude was his aunt. She gave us a grand time. Then on to Riga and Reval. From there to Helsinki in Finland and Danzig in Poland. The exchange there was dead in our favour. You got an absolute wad of Polish money for an English pound. I remember we went out to Zopott, a rather gay resort, one night, where there was a casino and had a little gamble with our few pounds. Luck was dead with us. We won a packet!

"Then we went to Copenhagen and Gothenburg and back to Invergordon after a really lovely time. Just the thing to take his mind off the tragedy.

"In London I played squash with him at the old Bath Club every morning from eleven to midday and then we usually went on for lunch at the Ritz Grill—when we could afford it—because it was quiet and very few people there. 'P.G.' hated being stared at and pointed out to people.

"He never forgot his friends, however. When he went out to the China station I didn't see him for four years. Then I arrived in London one afternoon and went to the Bath Club—quite unannounced. There was a message waiting for me; 'Meet me at the Berkeley at seven o'clock tonight for a meal.' That was the sort of chap he was. He always kept track of one and never forgot a friend.

"He loved the sea but the sea didn't love him. He suffered from a constitutional digestive trouble which caused frightful bouts of sea-sickness. So he was forced to retire with the rank of Commander in 1929.

"He was attached then to the Foreign Office and, later, to the Home Office, so that he might get a first-hand insight into the work of State Departments. He ranked at the Home Office as a Factory Inspector and remarked, 'I'm the first one of the family to become a Civil Servant.' "

One way and another, he was the most travelled member of the Royal family after the Prince of Wales. He had a captivating, easy charm of manner.

Lord Charles Cavendish once said to me: "You've only to be with 'P.G.' for five minutes to feel that you're the only man in the room."

The man who could hunt, shoot, dance, collect china and pictures, adore the Russian ballet, play the piano and have a standing order with an East End music shop to supply him with every new piece of dance music was also the keenest motorist of the Royal family. He was one of the first men in Britain to install a radio set in his car.

To sum up, he was a man among princes, a prince among men and a man in any crowd. He had the good manners of the Royal family. Perhaps his first lesson in human values was given him as a small child by Queen Mary when they were walking one day in the woods near Balmoral. They met an old Scottish crofter's wife carrying a load of firewood.

"George," said Queen Mary, "carry those sticks for the lady."

That principle of quick, unobtrusive service endured throughout his life. He inherited his father's intolerance of fools, his father's down-rightness of character. He never shirked responsibility. He loved beauty. In Princess Marina he met the perfect complement to his own character, his own interests, his own love of music, painting and all beauty.

He was a member of the Brooklands Aero Club, a qualified pilot, and also a Mason. He was initiated into Masonry on April 13th, 1928, and was a Master Mason the following June.

He visited Norway to represent the King and Queen at King Haakon's twenty-fifth anniversary of accession in December, 1930, and then set out on his greatest adventure. The eighteen-thousand-mile tour of South America with the Prince of Wales.

Later, he visited South Africa. In Bechuanaland he astounded the natives and the white population alike by going for a five-mile run in the hot African sun with Len Richardson, an Olympic running champion. When Richardson suggested turning back, "P.G." put on more speed!

Native tribesmen gave him a fantastic welcome at Umtata in Cape Province where the chief of the Tembu tribe, black as coal, in silk hat and morning coat, striped trousers and spats, insisted on mounting the dais three times running and saluted "P.G." no less than two hundred and fifteen times.

When he got back from South Africa, his uncle, the Earl of Athlone, said, jokingly, at dinner:

"It's time you thought of getting married, you know."

Prince George said nothing. He already had his own thoughts on the matter.

A few months later, in August, 1934, he was dining with a friend. They talked of Princess Marina, that warm, impulsive, unrepressed, utterly natural young woman, essentially feminine, naturally beautiful, who had so impressed them both.

"You know, she's the one woman," said Prince George, "with whom I could be happy to spend the rest of my life." He stopped, as though feeling he had said too much. Then he added, with the Englishman's recoil against sentiment: "We laugh at the same sort of things. She beats me at most games. And she doesn't care a damn how fast I drive when I take her out in a car."

He went down to Cowes. He heard that she was staying in Munich with her sister, Countess Toerring, and that she was going on from there to stay with her elder sister, Princess Olga and her husband, Prince Paul, at their log-cabin chalet at Bohinj, set on the shores of an enchanted lake, high in the Julian Alps, in that old, story-tale, feudal land of Slovenia.

He suddenly made up his mind, cancelled all engagements. He had a standing invitation to stay at Bohinj. So he wired Prince Paul that he would arrive about August 16th. Then he moved fast. He borrowed the Prince of Wales's private plane, took off, first stop Le Bourget, and flew on at such top-speed that he landed on the Yugoslav aerodrome at Ljubljana ahead of time. Prince Paul had not even had time to get there to meet him. So he took a car and drove out over the mountain road through resinous pine-woods, through the mountain stillness in the haze of an August afternoon, until he came to the wooden chalet by the lake-side with its outside staircases, its balconies, gables and Hans Andersen air.

Princess Marina was on the terrace, "her arms full of flowers which she had just gathered in the garden, her golden-brown hair ruffled by the light breeze". She did not expect him so soon. She walked slowly towards him, her arms full of flowers. Those who saw had no doubt.

Her uncle, Prince Christopher, was at Bohinj when Prince George arrived with his equerry, Major Humphrey Butler, in the plane. He said: "It was the first time I'd seen George for some years and I was struck by his resemblance to his father at his age. He had the same habit of crinkling up his eyes when he smiled; his laugh was absolutely the King's."

Prince Christopher had been in Rome, a week or so before, when he suddenly got an urgent letter from Prince Paul of Yugoslavia. He wrote: "Get into the next train and come to Bohinj. We need your help with some very serious business."

Prince Christopher immediately telephoned his niece, Princess Olga, to ask her what it was all about.

"Marina is staying with us," she explained, "and George is coming out from England next week. You remember you were with us when Elizabeth got engaged to Toto (Count Toerring). They are both so happy that I have an idea that you will bring Marina luck too."

During the next few days Prince George and Princess Marina walked in the pine woods, swam in the lake, played tennis in the cool evening. The rest of the house party simmered.

On the evening of the fifth day they all played backgammon in the sitting-room until midnight. Then, gradually, everyone went to bed.

Said Prince Christopher:

"George and Marina were left sitting alone at opposite ends of the sofa.

"I had been in my bedroom for about half an hour when I discovered that I had left my cigarette case on the backgammon table. Putting on my dressing-gown I went in search of it.

"The door of the sitting-room was open. George and Marina were still seated on the sofa, no longer, I observed with satisfaction, at the opposite ends of it. I stole back to bed without my case.

"The next day their engagement was announced."

The engagement, long-rumoured, often denied, was described as "the best kept secret in Europe".

His naval friend and "bear leader" of the earlier days received a picture-postcard from Salzburg showing a moonlit bay with the moon high in the sky. On it "P.G." had written; "I've done it! I can't tell you how happy I am."

When Prince George flew off from London on August 15th in that year of 1934, not even his own Comptroller, Major Ulick Alexander, knew what was in his mind. The only member of the Royal family who had been let into the secret was his eldest brother, the Prince of Wales.

Ulick Alexander said: "The announcement came as a complete surprise to me."

So it did to the citizens of not only London but of Salzburg where Prince George and Princess Marina and the rest of the family party stayed at the Hotel de L'Europe just after the announcement of the engagement.

The *Daily Mail* was the first newspaper to tell Salzburg the news. This newspaper telephoned the manager of the hotel and told him.

"We have heard rumours," he said, "but yours is the first definite information. The Royal party have been out all day but they are back now. Prince George is sitting with Princess Marina in the hotel lounge.

"They both look extremely happy and tonight the Princess looks more beautiful than I have ever seen her look before.

"Your charming Prince has captured the hearts of us all here and we are happy that he has so lovely a bride-to-be."

Prince Nicholas's own equerry said at the time:

"Prince George had sent a telegram to Prince Paul from Cowes asking if he might come. When he arrived we had no idea that he would propose marriage to Princess Marina but within five days of his arrival he did so.

"It was a great surprise to everyone here except perhaps those two most intimately involved."

Prince Nicholas, her father, interviewed, said:

"My wife and I are delighted at the news of the engagement. We are both very much attached to England and so is Marina who is delighted at the prospect of going to live there. There is nothing political in the marriage. It is one of affection."

The one ungracious comment came from Venizelos, the upstart dictator who sprang from nowhere and died utterly discredited, the man who ruined the Greek Royal family. He had the impertinence to say:

"I am convinced this wedding has no political significance. It is the most natural thing in the world for two young people to fall in love. If I thought the marriage had any political import I should say more."

Here, at home in England, King George V and Queen Mary were wholeheartedly delighted at the prospect of welcoming such a charming, natural and accomplished daughter-in-law. A tremendous wave of joy swept Britain. The romance caught the popular fancy. It captured the heart of the man, and the woman, in the street. Here were a Prince and Princess Charming who actually looked, and acted, the parts of that overworked phrase.

A shoal of telegrams from Royalties, exiled and otherwise, Lord Mayors, Mayors, State officials, Members of both Houses of Parliament, from Clubs, Societies, Associations and from humble people who wired their congratulations simply because they felt they must, poured into the log-chalet at Bohinj and the Hotel de L'Europe at Salzburg.

At the latter place, Prince George and his fiancée spent the next few days shopping during the morning, walking in the pine-woods, listening to the music of the Salzburg Festival. He drove her about on the first day of their arrival in an open car, dressed in a chalk-stripe, grey flannel, double-breasted suit and cap. She wore a tailor-made suit and a grey beret and carried a bunch of white roses. He signed the hotel register as "George, Prince von England". She signed as "Marina, Prinzessin von Greichenland und Danemark," August 27th, 1934.

They shared the same hotel suite with Prince Paul and Princess Olga.

Amidst the wave of rejoicing which swept the British Empire, perhaps the oddest little celebration of all took place in the Tokio Club. There a little group of British Naval officers, merchants and others raised their glasses to a signed chit for drinks which hung framed above the bar. It bore Prince George's signature. They had "wangled" it out of him when he visited the club as a Naval officer and was persuaded to toss for drinks all round. They had arranged beforehand for him to lose!

I like that little vignette, as much as the other picture of the simple welcome which the lovers received from the villagers at Bohinj.

They all trooped up to the chalet to congratulate them, headed by the village mayor. The men wore feathered hats and embroidered waistcoats. The women were in large petticoats and loose, white linen blouses embroidered in bright reds, yellows and blues. They wore their national head-dresses of goffered muslin, hanging far down their backs, and piled high on their heads in vast, starched bows. The young girls wore flowers and ribbons.

This picturesque procession, a cameo from the older Europe, walked up to the house headed by fiddlers fiddling like mad, others playing concertinas. They marched through the garden and on to a grassy bank before the terrace. There they sang—like larks and nightingales.

Hand in hand, the Royal couple came out of the house and stood on the terrace. A shower of flowers descended on them. A tiny girl with flaxen pigtails marched forward with a wreath of red roses. She stopped in front of Princess Marina and looked up at her shyly, hesitating. Then her mother, a laughing country girl, ran forward, snatched her up and lifted the chuckling child high in the air so that she could place the red wreath on Princess Marina's head.

Then Princess Marina kissed the little pig-tailed girl and patted her cheeks.

Next, two handsome village girls came forward with bouquets. Blue cornflowers and white edelweiss for Princess Marina, and red roses for Prince George—the Royal coronation colours of red, white and blue.

A storm of cheers and lusty huzzas from the crowd. "Jiva Marina! Jiva Georg!" (Long live Marina! Long live George!) Then the whole procession threw flowers at the feet of the blushing and slightly embarrassed couple. Neither could speak Yugoslav! Luckily Prince Paul came to their rescue. He thanked the mayor and thanked the villagers and announced that he was sending barrels of beer down to the village for them to drink the health of the engaged couple.

The mayor, in reply, said that the village had decided to re-name a street after Prince George. They only hoped that he and his bride would come back to visit Bohinj once again.

Vivid and overwhelming contrast awaited Princess Marina when she returned to Paris. The railway station was packed with a seething mass of people. The platform was walled by police. They had to cordon off a passage for the Royal couple. Newspapermen, Press cameras and newsreel cameras besieged them. Princess Marina shrank back from it all in sudden alarm. "I have never yet made a picture for the camera," she said. Prince George took her by the hand, led her forward.

The girl who had lived eleven years as an unknown exile came back to a Paris which put her on a sudden, dazzling pedestal. People who had avoided her family for years flocked round her. Invitations poured in from those who had studiously ignored them while Prince Nicholas was painting for a living and the family was living quietly in the comparatively modest flat in the Avenue Henri Martin.

Doors shut to them as exiles opened with a splendid flourish to the girl about to marry into the leading Royal house of Europe.

Prince Nicholas was indignant. Princess Marina, the soul of charity, merely laughed: "Darling, what *does* it matter? Would you expect people to behave otherwise?"

Her mind flew back to Athens where they had been cheered and fêted one day, showered with insults and abuse the next. Life had taught her some of its bitterest lessons.

The next visit was to England to meet her future father-in-law and mother-in-law, King George V and Queen Mary. She was the first foreigner to marry into the Royal house of England since her own great-aunt, Queen Alexandra, had gone there as a Princess of Denmark. The Queen who had told her: "Remember, my dear, the English are the most loyal friends in the world if once you win their hearts but there are no half-measures with them."

When she arrived on a Sunday with her parents at the Gare du Nord *en route* for England, the platform was a sea of heads. They almost had to fight their way to the barrier.

In that mêlée Princess Marina noticed, among the crowd, a little group of laughing and chattering work-girls from the fashion-house which made her clothes. They had worked overtime all through the week to finish the dresses she was taking to England. Now they were giving up their Sunday holiday to see her off.

She went straight over, talked with them all, and thanked them most charmingly before getting into the carriage.

Just as the train was about to start a young man burst through the crowd at the barrier, sent a couple of railway officials spinning on their heels, dashed up to the Princess's compartment and thrust what looked like a sodden newspaper into her hands. It was a small bunch of dahlias wrapped up in *Le Matin*.

Princess Marina recognized him as one of the many Russian refugee orphans who had been fed, clad, housed and educated in the children's home at St. Germain which her mother had set up. There she had bathed the babies, put them to bed, soothed the fractious and told bed-time stories to the small people who refused to go to sleep without them. Here, at the last second of departure, was a face from those days.

Her carriage was piled with orchids, roses and carnations. As the train steamed out she held in her hand that one pathetic bunch of dahlias—the human echo of the years of exile.

CHAPTER EIGHT

The Wedding

ON THAT bright autumn day when Princess Marina crossed the Channel and saw, on the skyline, the white cliffs of Sussex, the green horizon of the Downs, the land of Harold the Saxon and William the Mamser, she left behind the shattered dynastic hopes of her own family, the bright-eyed upstanding Danes who had tried to make a kingdom out of Greece. She came back, on the slow turn of the wheel of history, to the Isles which the Danes themselves had conquered a thousand years before. She was returning to her own.

In such a style but with no background of death and bitterness, her great-aunt, Princess Alexandra of Denmark, had sailed to England seventy-one years earlier when she became the bride of Edward, Prince of Wales, later Edward VII of England, "The Peacemaker".

Thus, history repeated itself.

When they landed at Folkestone the docks and quayside were black with people. England had risen to her feet. The bright clear skies of Channel blue, rang with the lusty shouts of Kentish men and women. It was a homecoming for a bride in the old, human way of history.

The Mayor was there. The Councillors were there. The Men of State from London were there. The Royal relations were there. Flags flew and the cheers put the gulls to squalling flight.

Among the crowd, as the ship edged her way gingerly alongside the wooden bulwarks of the quay, there stood out one quiet solid, homely, figure—a white-haired woman with an English face. The eternal governess.

"Foxy." Dear devoted "Foxy" who had nursed Marina from a child, disciplined her, trained her, been cast bitterly from her when slander, murder and abdication ruined her family.

"Foxy" returned that day, unobtrusive, loyal, devoted. The moment of triumphant home-coming, to the new home which, after all, was not so very new in terms of history for any Princess of the Viking blood.

Those who waited ashore to see the ship which bore to England the Princess who had caught the heart of the world, saw a slim, girlish figure in rust-red suddenly break into a beaming smile and wave furiously to an old lady, shrinking in the background. The ultimate symbol of British solidity and trust—her nanny.

When the train drew into Victoria the station was packed. Inside and outside, crowds waited. Police, in dark blue lines, marshalled the patient Londoners who had come to see their new and glamorous Princess.

Against that background of tense, curious faces, Prince George waited. Tall, fresh-faced, young—the man on whom all eyes dwelt.

Princess Marina stepped from her carriage, poised, cool and yet a little shy. A subdued wave of clapping.

Prince George stepped forward and kissed her—rather shyly. And the sudden thunder of cheers lifted the roof.

Outside the station people lined the route from Victoria to York House, St. James's. Banners flew. Bunting fluttered. Children wagged flags. Women threw flowers in front of the car. Men raised their hats and waved their umbrellas. London, the ancient, undemonstrative city, had suddenly taken her to its own warm heart.

Outside York House a sea of faces surged in Cleveland Court, beneath the tall windows of the Prince's bachelor suite.

"We want Marina! We want the Princess!"

The chant rolled like thunder.

She came to the open window, Prince George beside her, with his Alsatian, "Doushka". Her hat was off. The wind ruffled her fair brown hair. She put up a slim hand to pat her hair into place. The crowd saw the flash of a ring on her third finger.

"What stone is it?" someone shouted.

"It's a sapphire," she cried with a girlish laugh. She turned her hand from side to side so that the crowd could see it.

That instinctive gesture of a young woman proud of her lover, proud of her new ring, utterly charmed the crowd. She had conquered London.

That night they went up to Balmoral on the sleeper.

Dawn broke over ancient hills, the wide sweep of purple moors, the clean dawn of a young, Scottish day. It looked, in its glassy clarity, so like the classic hills of faraway Greece.

The little station at Ballater was bright with bunting, flags and flowers. The Royal Guard of the Argyll and Sutherland Highlanders, swagger in kilts, glinting with silver resplendent, snapped to attention.

Thus her father's beloved Evzoni, the kilted Greek Highlanders, had sprung to attention when she had gone to Tatoi. Here were the same pine-woods, the everlasting hills, the resin-scent on the wind. It was the same happy atmosphere of a loving family.

Then by car to Balmoral, that pepper-pot castle, Scots baronial, perched above the sliding shallows of the Dee between the eternal purple of the moors, the stillness of fir-woods, the singing of a salmon river in the stillness of night.

It had the eternal quality of the Grecian highlands. The ancient gods walk always upon the hills. Here was, as Charles Edward Stuart and John Sobieski had sung, a hundred years before . . .

> "The ridge of hinds, the steep of the sloping glens
> The wood of cuckoos at its foot
> The blue height of a thousand pines
> Of wolves, and roes and elks."

Without the wolves, it was all so like Tatoi. So like the old, beloved mountains of Greece. The same marching pines against the sky. Sailing clouds. The sea-wind in the trees. The night-talk of the river over the stones. And by day in the blue silences:

> "Lone sanctuaries where we have said
> The gods have been, the gods may be."

Mountains have always bred poets and chivalry. The kilts of the Highlanders and the wild mountain music of the bagpipes which moaned and skirled under the dark heights of Lochnagar were little different from the swinging kilts of those beloved Evzoni who had guarded Tatoi and wept when she left, whose bagpipes had piped the music that Daphnis and Chloe knew when they lived and loved their idyll, eighteen centuries before in the mountain groves of Mitylene.

The Duchess of York, now the Queen Mother, came over from Birkhall and taught Princess Marina how to dance Highland reels—not so far removed from the mountain dances of the shepherds of Greece.

"I was enchanted," said Princess Marina, "by one thing more than all else—the ghillies' ball. There the servants dance with the Royal family without any sense of familiarity but with the utmost good friendship."

That, to her, brought up in the unselfconscious atmosphere of the

Greek Royal family with their down-to-earth commonsense principles of leadership was a return to the values of her childhood. True monarchy is always the truest democracy.

From Balmoral back to London—that city which is no city but a great congregation of villages, each proud of itself, a sprawl of roofs beside the Thames. A place of masts and tall chimneys, of green parks and shining waters. A city of smoke and splendour. The citadel of monarchy and the middle class.

Dominated, in its own, quiet way, by the domestic whiteness of Whitehall, the broad avenue of the Mall, the grey magnificence of Buckingham Palace, the splendour of the Royal Standard against the western sky.

London loved, on sight, this bride-to-be of the youngest son of the King of England. The last great splendid monarchy that had survived, not by any mystic archaism, nor by mailed fist or double-headed eagle, not by the tendentious culture of a Roi Soleil but by the sheer fact that it is the kingdom of an ancient, thinking people whose kings long since learned how to govern. The tall, cool girl with the air of grace and Royal dignity, the flash of humour, the classic grace, was of that pattern. She belonged.

From Balmoral, Princess Marina went back to London for a week's shopping and then to Paris. Her trousseau was the talking point of the day. Where would she order it? The Paris house of Molyneux which had always dressed her hoped she would go to them. London hoped that the future British Princess would buy it there. Russian refugees naturally hoped that, for the daughter of a Russian Grand Duchess, they would have a hand in its making.

The order was given to the Paris house of Captain Molyneux, who was an Englishman in any case, with the stipulation that some dresses should be made from English material and that as many Russian refugees as possible should be given work in making the dresses.

In the midst of these wedding preparations and, tragically, on the actual day on which Prince George was created Duke of Kent, that kindly man, King Alexander of Yugoslavia, was assassinated by a Communist within a few moments of landing at Marseilles on a State visit to France.

Princess Marina, who was a cousin of the young widowed Queen Mignon, at once went to Belgrade for the funeral. Prince George flew there to represent King George V.

Tragedy, which had followed her through childhood and young

womanhood, a long, bitter tale of murder, assassination and exile, had struck at her family yet again, almost on the eve of her own wedding.

Prince George, now Duke of Kent, stayed for a few days on his way home to England with Princess Marina and her family in the flat off the Avenue Henri Martin. He visited Prince Nicholas's studio and saw his paintings. He went shopping in Paris with Princess Marina, travelling by bus and Tube as she had always done. He shared their simple family meal, and in those few days he learned more, perhaps, of her united and utterly devoted home-life than he had ever known before.

The wedding was fixed for November 29th, 1934. A specially chartered ship brought Princess Marina and her family to England nine days before. They were guests at Buckingham Palace. The Duke of Kent had already taken Lady Juliet Duff's house, furnished, at No. 3 Belgrave Square, with a free hand to re-decorate in any way they liked.

Meanwhile, wedding presents poured into the Duke's apartments at St. James's Palace.

It was typical of Princess Marina's thoughtfulness for the poor and needy, particularly children, that she should issue the following announcement:

"I would like the people of England to share in some way my great happiness on the occasion of my engagement to Prince George. As you know, my years of exile have taught me how much unhappiness there is in the world. Although I should be happy to think that the preparations for my wedding were in some small measure giving employment to those who need it, I should be more than happy for the unemployed, and particularly for their children, to receive any money which has been intended for the purchase of wedding gifts for me."

On a bleak, November evening a verger waited alone at a side door in Westminster Abbey. The last notes of evensong had died away. The last sightseers had gone out into the mist. The Abbey was alone with its ghosts.

The side door opened quietly. A tall young man with a girl in a fur coat, stepped quietly inside. The verger recognized the beautiful oval face with the glowing eyes under a little, tight-fitting hat of curling ostrich plumes. Princess Marina and the Duke of Kent.

They walked quietly with the verger into the muted silence of that

Family group in the garden at Coppins—the Duke of Kent with Prince
Edward and the Duchess with Princess Alexandra (portrait by Cecil Beaton,
1941)

The Duke and Duchess of Kent with their youngest child, Prince Michael,
then six weeks old—photographed by Cecil Beaton at Coppins ten days before
the Duke's death

The Duchess with her children, 1947

old and splendid church. The last evening light glowed through tall, stained windows, faintly.

For a few moments, they knelt before the High Altar in silent prayer. For the next day they were, there, to be made man and wife.

The London crowds were already gathered outside Buckingham Palace when they drove back on that night of November 28th. The King and Queen were giving a great State banquet. More than forty Royalties, Kings, Queens, Princesses and Grand Duchesses of every dynasty in Europe were there. The splendours of the Edwardian Age came to life again. There had been no banquet like it since 1914.

The white-and-gold State Room, the glitter of gold plate. The magnificence of jewels, the brilliance of uniforms, made a picture whose like could not be reproduced in any Court in Europe. It was the first time Princess Marina had been at such a banquet. The first time, indeed, that she had stayed at Buckingham Palace on a State occasion. The new world opened its splendid doors—a vista of happiness and vast responsibilities.

After the banquet the Duke and Princess Marina toured the West End just before midnight to see the decorations. They were mobbed by a crowd of more than 5,000 people in Piccadilly Circus.

She woke next morning at 7 a.m. From her bedroom window the Mall already glittered with long lines of motor-cars, the pavements black with waiting people. England was afoot early on that November morning. London was electric with excitement. More than a hundred special trains brought visitors from the provinces. Whole families picnicked early in St. James's Park, Green Park and Hyde Park, eating their breakfasts on the damp autumn grass so that they might be in time to see the bride go by.

In Buckingham Palace preparations ran like clockwork. The white-and-gold ballroom glowed with flowers for the wedding breakfast. The kitchen staff were up before daybreak. The wedding cake, nine feet high, weighing 600 pounds, baked in Edinburgh, packed with lucky gold charms, stood on a table waiting to be cut.

Princess Marina was attended in her room at 9 a.m. by her hairdresser, Monsieur Grande of Paris. Originally her coiffure was to consist of small, tight curls at the back of her head, the hair taken straight back from the forehead. It was found at the last minute that these curls upset the "line" of the veil so they were changed for smooth coils.

Her old nanny, "dear Foxy", helped her into the wedding dress.

7

Designed by Molyneux in silver French brocade, made in Lyons, woven with English roses of medieval design, it was the sort of dress an English princess would have worn in the Middle Ages. The sleeves widened from shoulder to wrist, the cuffs faced with silver brocade. The flowing, billowing white tulle veil was five feet long, widening at the bottom to ten feet. Holding this in place was a magnificent diamond tiara presented to Princess Marina by the City of London. She wore two small bunches of orange blossom over each ear.

The material for the dress was so delicate that it was only sent over to England about two weeks before the wedding.

Against the fog and dampness of London, Princess Marina wore a white ermine wrap over her dress.

Her bouquet was of lilies, carnations and orchids, all white, grown in the Royal gardens at Windsor. Incorporated in it was a sprig of myrtle, part of every English Royal bride's bouquet. It was plucked from a tree grown for Queen Victoria.

Princess Marina wore a diamond necklace and long white gloves.

In accordance with Royal custom the veil was worn back from the face. This dates from ancient times when there was some danger of a Royal bride being substituted by someone else.

Meanwhile, in York House, St. James's Palace, the Duke of Kent, dressing himself in full Naval uniform, made the startling discovery that he had only a few shillings in his pocket. Not the style in which to start a honeymoon.

So he walked through the packed crowds, went to his bank, cashed a cheque and walked back again. Not a soul recognized him!

The Prince of Wales, who was to be best man, and the Duke of York, arrived to find their brother pushing his way through the crowd outside St. James's Palace.

"Surely you could have sent someone to the bank," they expostulated.

"Oh! Easily," he said. "But it gave me something to do."

Outside the bells of London rang from reeling spires. The bells of Westminster Abbey were rung in a full peal of no less than 5,040 changes, an astonishing performance seldom heard by the citizens of London.

Elsewhere Union Jacks and Greek flags, long, fluttering strings of bunting, huge coloured bells, glittering galaxies of lights and innumerable Greek and British crowns intertwined, beautified the streets and gave the waiting thousands a free display of gaiety and colour.

The crush in the streets was so great that first-aid stations were set up outside the Ritz and elsewhere for people who had fainted. Many had been up all night or sleeping in doorways and under arches on camp-beds with thermos flasks and blankets.

When Princess Marina left Buckingham Palace in a glass coach, pale as marble in her white dress of silver, in a cloud of white tulle, crowned by a glittering tiara of diamonds, her loveliness was not of this world. The crowd gasped. Then arose a thunder of cheers seldom heard in the sedate streets of London. It continued in a wave of sound, a surge of fluttering hands and hats, all the way to the Abbey. And, over all, the bells clashed and pealed.

Prince Christopher, who drove through vast crowds of people who had waited all through the night, wrote in his diary:

"They were profoundly touching in their wonderful enthusiasm. Only in England now, I think, do you find this personal love of the Sovereign and his family, a sentiment that surpasses even fidelity; a perfect understanding that makes even the poorest subject feel that he has a right to share in the joys and sorrows of the Royal family. . . .

"Watching those dense crowds I found myself remembering what King George had said so many years before: 'It is one of the greatest responsibilities on earth to be the ruler of the British people. They trust one so implicitly.' "

Inside the Abbey the Archbishop of Canterbury, Dr. Lang, the Archbishop of York, Dr. Temple, and the Dean of Westminster, Dr. Foxley Norris, waited in the medieval splendour of their vestments.

Royalties who had known the power and majesty of pre-war years; Ministers of State; generals in scarlet; admirals glittering with gold braid; peeresses splendid with jewels; ambassadors; Members of Parliament and men-at-arms in scarlet, carrying pikes, made a dramatic backdrop of colour.

In the solemn splendour of the Abbey pale shafts of November light, through stained windows, lit the gilded reredos of the altar, where vessels of gold glowed, candles flickered.

In that dim place of majestic peace the blue and gold, scarlet and silver of uniforms and shining swords, gave a dignity and splendour which the dull trappings of a Republic could never match.

A man and woman, each of old and Royal blood, were about to marry.

"Gracious Spirit, Holy Ghost . . ." The strains echoed down the Abbey—the bride was coming. A rustle of expectation went through that audience of four thousand people. The King, in the full-dress uniform of an Admiral of the Fleet, turned his head. Queen Mary, royal in blue and silver, bent forward to see better. Little Princess Margaret Rose, only four years old and bubbling with excitement, bobbed up and down on a footstool at the feet of the Duchess of York. The bridegroom looked round shyly.

There, slowly, up the aisle, on the arm of her father, Prince Nicholas of Greece, came the bride, infinitely lovely, girlishly regal, her dress and train a cloud of white and silver. Before her trod the Canons. Behind her followed two small figures in knee-length frocks of stiff, white tulle over silver lamé, her train-bearers. They were Princess Elizabeth, the present Queen, and Lady May Cambridge. Their skirts were very full from the waist, belted by bands of silver and tiny white roses.

Behind them walked slowly the six bridesmaids, Princess Irene of Greece, tall, fair and lovely; the Grand Duchess Kira of Russia, strikingly fair; Princess Eugenie of Greece and Princess Katherine of Greece, all first cousins of the bride. The other two were Princess Juliana of Holland, the present Queen Juliana, and Lady Iris Mountbatten.

The bride walked slowly, her head bent slightly, a faint smile lighting those delicately classic features.

The Duke of Kent looked pale. As the bride took her place beside him they exchanged sudden, warm smiles.

"George Edward Alexander Edmund, wilt thou have this woman to be thy wedded wife?"

"I will." His voice rang out abruptly, plainly heard.

"Marina, wilt thou have this man to be thy wedded husband?"

"I will." Her voice was soft and low.

As they two spoke the marriage vows, people in all the far corners of the world heard them. Tears of gladness glistened in many eyes in many countries. Ancient loyalties and old, forgotten memories sprang to new life in the hearts of thousands who had known the splendour and the peace of the old days of monarchy in countries beyond the English seas. For this was the first Royal wedding in England ever to be broadcast to the world. They heard the Archbishop's words:

"You, sir, have already and fully taken your place in the service of the community. And you, dear bride, as your husband's comrade, will find a new happiness in sharing the joys and sorrows and in ministering to the needs of the good British folk who have already, with a warmth so swift and spontaneous, taken you into their hearts.

"I am sure that that heart is now speaking through my words as I say—God bless you both. God guide you. God keep you always."

Long years afterwards, many who listened, remembered that soft, half-afraid voice which said breathlessly: "I, Marina, take thee, George Edward Alexander Edmund, to my wedded husband . . . to love, cherish, and to obey, till death do us part."

Little they knew, in that high moment of supreme bliss, trust and faith, that the tragic fate which had dogged all too many of her family, loomed on the near horizon of the years.

The newly married couple went into the Chapel of St. Edward the Confessor to sign the register. They forgot the bride's bouquet of white lilies. Or rather, the Prince of Wales, who was best man, forgot it. He had already forgotten to hand the ring to the bridegroom at the crucial moment of the ceremony until the Queen noticed it, touched the King on the arm and he, in turn, signalled to the Prince of Wales!

Now he forgot to pick up her bouquet and the bridegroom's gloves, which all merely goes to show that Royal lovers and Royal brothers are as human as the rest of us when it comes to the ritual of a wedding.

When they came out of the Abbey and entered the glass coach to drive to Buckingham Palace, Lady Mary Hope (now Lady Herbert) Lady-in-Waiting to the new Duchess of Kent, saw that a hot-water bottle was put in, wrapped in a small white blanket, to keep the bride warm. November in London!

Then back to Buckingham Palace where a second marriage ceremony was gone through in the tiny, red-carpeted private chapel. There the Greek Archbishop, Doctor Strinopoulos Germanos, performed the picturesque ceremony of the Greek Orthodox Church, a ceremony more than a thousand years old.

Only once before had a double wedding been held in the British Royal family. That was when the late Duke of Edinburgh married the Grand Duchess Marie of Russia, daughter of the Tsar Alexander II.

Then the wedding breakfast was served in the superb white-and-gold supper room of Buckingham Palace, fragrant with flowers. As the King and Queen entered with the newly-wed couple, the band played the National Anthem. When it ended the Duke led his bride to the top of the table to the bridal march from *Lohengrin*.

This was the wedding breakfast menu:

  Filet de Sole
  Côtes d'Agneau Braisées
  Perdreaux à la crême
  Pêches Melba
  Corbeilles de Friandises

There were toasts, jokes, good wishes and happiness.

Then the Duke and Duchess cut the first slice of the nine-foot high wedding cake with the Duke's sword.

She changed into a going-away dress of green wool, trimmed with brown nutria fur with a turban hat in green velvet, with diamond ear-rings and mink coat. As they got into the honeymoon coach and clattered off with an escort of Life Guards, a family party rushed across the inner quadrangle and showered tiny silver horseshoes and miniature wedding-bells over them.

The coach rumbled off amid laughter and cheers. A honeymoon lay ahead.

There is an odd quirk, a comic aside to almost every wedding. Prince Christopher of Greece tells a story of his niece's wedding which adds the final touch of modern humour. After the wedding reception was over he drove from Buckingham Palace to St. James's Palace to see the presents. He says:

"My wife was tired and unable to accompany me, so I had an imposing Royal car all to myself. In this I progressed, inch by inch, one of a long line of carriages filled with guests, along the Mall. Crowds lined the route, commenting with embarrassing frankness upon each car and its occupants, and my solitary state was a topic of general inquiry.

"I was getting quite used to hearing: 'Here's one all by himself. What swank!' when a wit in the front row of spectators varied it with: 'Here's Charlie Chaplin himself.' I protruded my domed head and horn-rimmed spectacles from the window. . . . 'Not at all,' I said, 'you're quite wrong this time. As a matter of fact, it's Harold Lloyd! . . . A roar of laughter went up!"

The wedding presents, which Prince Christopher was on his way to see, included a diamond tiara, ear-rings, a three-row pearl necklace with diamond clasps which the Duke gave to his bride, whilst she gave him a set of ruby cuff-links and a pig-skin and gold pocket case.

The bridesmaids' gifts were diamond brooches set in platinum with aquamarines with the initials G and M engraved on the backs. Other gifts to the Royal couple included two ostrich feather bedcovers, scent, a magnificent set of sapphire and diamond tiara, necklace and bracelets from the Queen, furniture, clocks, jewellery, antiques, sixty pairs of gloves from the Worshipful Company of Glovers, lingerie and bedjackets.

The first part of the honeymoon was spent at Himley Hall, the Earl of Dudley's vast and somewhat rococo seat in Staffordshire, since pulled down. Then they spent a little time at Trent Park, Sir Philip Sassoon's place near Barnet; Christmas at Sandringham; a visit to her sister and brother-in-law, Count and Countess Toerring-Jettenbach, in Bavaria, and wound up with a cruise to the West Indies.

There, at Nassau, the Duke and Duchess met President Roosevelt. He was cruising in Vincent Astor's yacht. He was attracted by the young couple and asked them to luncheon with him.

Franklin Roosevelt was a man of strong likes and dislikes, instant impressions. The Duke and Duchess were unlike the American idea of British Royalty. Their youth, vitality and democratic outlook appealed to him.

"Come and see me in Washington," he invited.

"I'd love to. I'll fly over some day," the Duke promised.

Years later, after the Second World War had plunged the nations into a new barbarity, the Duke flew the Atlantic in a Liberator bomber when we needed the utmost American goodwill. Roosevelt welcomed him. That honeymoon visit to Jamaica did this nation immense good in those dark years when goodwill and personal trust with the President of the United States meant everything.

That is why, today, Prince Michael, third child of the Duchess of Kent, bears also the Christian name of Franklin.

CHAPTER NINE

Belgrave Square and Coppins

NUMBER THREE Belgrave Square is one of those tall, white, stately houses which Cubitt, the great nineteenth-century builder, put up for the Grosvenor Estates in the last century. It looks south over that noble square which, with the wide streets and other squares about it, were marshland pastures, snipe-haunted, until an Act was passed for their drainage in 1826. Then the buttercup fields of the Manor of Ebury were transformed, within a few years, into Belgravia by the wealth and wisdom of Hugh, Lord Belgrave, later first Duke of Westminster.

Number Three belonged to Lady Juliet Duff, an Edwardian hostess with all the vigour of her Lowther blood. She let it furnished to the Kents with the provision that they could re-decorate or re-furnish as they pleased.

The Duke loved good furniture and pictures. His sense of decorative values was so sure that he could order silks, brocades, chintzes and colours with the eye and appreciation of a woman. In him, the almost-forgotten good taste of the eighteenth century lived again. The Duchess admired and trusted his discrimination. So, when he began to buy furniture and plan decorations, she collaborated enthusiastically.

Thus the tall, white house with its sunny rooms, large and high, became, within a few months, a treasure house of their own things.

The Duchess chose the colours for most of the rooms. Thereby she popularized a new colour-tone which became known as "blonde". It really amounted to a combination of light pastel shades with a blonde predominance.

The hall was in grey-blonde. A brown stair-carpet with a silver sheen in it and bowls of Madonna lilies or pink azaleas set off this colour-tone perfectly.

The blonde motif continued in some of the Duchess's own rooms whilst the Duke's bedroom has been described to me as a "green-blonde" whatever that may be. Off-white dominated other rooms.

For the nursery, a large, bright room, they chose blue and white chintzes and a rug worked in nursery rhymes. They had quite made

During the war the Duchess was much occupied with the special duties which faced all members of the Royal family. She is here seen with a group of women factory workers, and as Commandant W.R.N.S. on a visit to Dover where she took a look at occupied France

(*Opposite*) Philip de Laszlo's portrait of Princess Nicholas provides a background to this photograph of her daughter

(*Above*) The Duchess with her son the second Duke of Kent, photographed on the eve of their departure for the Far East in 1952
(both photographs by Cecil Beaton)

Child welfare has always been one of the Duchess's interests: a visit to a Babies' Club in Chelsea

Viewing her own portrait of her sister Princess Olga at the exhibition of the Society of Women Artists, 1952

up their minds that their first child would be a boy. So had Queen Mary. She and the Duchess stocked the toy cupboard with boys' toys and tied blue ribbons on the cot weeks before the baby was expected.

When, in the early hours of October 9th, 1935, the young Prince Edward, now Duke of Kent, finally arrived, the secretary's room downstairs was packed with reporters.

London that night was agog to hear the news. The "romantic Duchess" as the Americans called her, had completely captured the nation's heart. Her first baby was an Event.

Just before midnight the door opened. A pale and rather haggard young man looked in and said to the reporters:

"I just thought I'd tell you that some hot coffee is being sent in to you. After that I'm afraid the kitchens will be closed but there'll be someone on duty just after six who will get you some breakfast." It was the Duke of Kent.

As he was going out of the door, he turned and, with that warm smile of his, said: "I do hope it'll be over soon. I don't think I could stand much more of this."

It was the human touch. The newspaper men respected it. Not one printed it.

A few days after the baby's arrival, Princess Margaret, then a small girl, was allowed a peep. She gazed at it solemnly, her eyes popping, and then asked, very seriously: "Is it real?" She prodded one tiny hand cautiously. "You're sure it won't break?"

The present Duke of Kent's fondness for cars blossomed early. As soon as he could speak one of the first words was "car". He repeated it through every shade of meaning—anticipation, pleading, frustration, longing, and, finally, sheer determination, until he was taken out in the car. Then he repeated the word joyfully, time and time again.

At four he could take a toy motor-car to pieces and re-assemble it. He had inherited his father's mechanical mind. Father and son spent hours together tinkering in the garage. When the small Prince went to stay with his grandparents at Sandringham he spent half his time in the fields watching farm tractors at work.

"I love Sandringham, Nanny," he confided solemnly to his nurse. "It's just like Heaven, one tractor after another."

It is said that when Prince Edward went into hospital to have his tonsils removed, the Duchess went to the hospital and bathed and put him to bed herself. After the operation she spent every afternoon reading to him or drawing comic strips which were passed round to other children in the hospital. The Duke always called to take her home and to have half an hour with his son. The latter was invariably full of questions.

"How many bricks are there in the hospital, Mummy?" he asked urgently one day. The Duchess had not the faintest idea. Neither had the matron. The latter, however, had to telephone the architects on other business so she asked them. They had no idea either.

Later that night when the matron entered Prince Edward's room, he squealed triumphantly: "I know how many bricks there are in this building. My father"—who was reading to him at that moment—"has just told me. He knows everything!" As the Duke was leaving the hospital that night the matron asked how he had found out the number of bricks in the building. "I didn't," he grinned, "but for Heaven's sake don't tell my son that I'm a liar."

Prince Edward was followed by his sister, Princess Alexandra, on December 25th, 1936, and, six years later, on July 4th, 1942, Prince Michael entered the world. It was an odd coincidence that the latter's birthday, July 4th, should be celebrated in the United States as Independence Day, since Prince Michael was christened Franklin after President Roosevelt, the first baby in the Royal family to be named after an American President.

The Duke and Duchess were devoted parents. Their children were the end-all and be-all of their private lives. One of the first toys which the Duke bought for little Prince Edward, when he was scarcely more than a year old, was a fascinating yellow plush cat with green eyes. They blazed as if by magic when the cat was squeezed. An electric battery inside lit the eyes when you squeezed the cat or pulled its tail. This he kept in his own room. The Duchess kept in her bedroom a "very special" teddy-bear with which Prince Edward played whenever he entered the room.

During this period the Duchess definitely established herself as the leader of London fashion. She influenced dress, decoration, and the textile industry as no other woman has done in this century.

"Marina" hats, those little pill-box affairs which she wore with such rare effect, swept England. "Marina blue" became the fashionable colour. She introduced the Edwardian hairstyle in the 1930s. She was the first member of the Royal family to wear the "New Look" in 1948. It caught on instantly.

Everything she said, did, or wore, was copied. Thanks to her the hideous craze for chromium-plated furniture and dazzle patterns in cushions and hangings, which made thousands of homes hideous, was killed. Her casual remark: "I would not like my house to look like a bar," slew that utterly indefensible phase of jazzed-up ugliness.

The mere fact that she never produced a powder-compact or lipstick, still less a comb, when she was dining in a restaurant or a night-club was enough to banish the slovenly habit among many young women of making up their faces, or even combing their hair, at the dining table.

When she pushed her own son in his pram round Belgrave Square and walked with him hand-in-hand on the lawns, other young mothers in Society decided that it might be just as well if they became a little more maternal also.

Above all, the Duchess by sheer force of example, did enormous good to the British textile and fashion trade.

At that time there was heavy depression and unemployment in Lancashire. The Duke, with his practical experience of industrial problems, told her of the desperate poverty of many work-people in the North. He urged her to popularize Lancashire cottons. She did so.

She asked her dressmaker to design cotton frocks for her. She wore them all that summer. Smart women, who would not have been seen dead in cotton, immediately followed her. Cotton became the rage. Manufacturers and designers produced better cottons, better designs. Today women can thank the Duchess for the enchanting cottons which are universal summer wear.

Equally she popularized Nottingham lace and Scotch tweed.

When she went on the Malayan tour in 1952 she took a great many cotton dresses with her. "Up to that time no smart woman would have been seen dead in a cotton dress," I was told by one who was on that tour. "The Duchess wore cotton, and cotton became the rage." Equally she started the vogue for big picture hats on State occasions.

The fact is that the Duchess not only knows how to dress and how to *wear* a dress but she never minds being seen in the same dress several times. She makes the dress. It does not *make* her.

Thus life went on in those few years at Belgrave Square. Young, gay, hard-working and full of plans for the future.

"If you want to see two completely happy people, you need only

spend a few minutes with my niece Marina and her husband." Thus
Prince Christopher of Greece to a friend when he was staying with the
Kents in 1938. And he added:

"Everyone seems to fall in love round George and Marina. I suppose
it's their example."

It was true. Within two years of their own marriage, Lord Herbert,
the Duke's equerry, married Lady Mary Hope, who was Lady-in-
Waiting to the Duchess. Then Mr. John Lowther, the Duke's secretary,
got married. It was catching.

So was hard work.

Ten days at Holyrood Palace meant meeting a thousand guests and
shaking hands with most of them, for the Duke was High Commissioner of the Church of Scotland. Ten days on their toes.

Then endless visits to industrial areas. Unemployment was a black
curse on England. Depression hit the North and Midlands hard. The
Duke, an expert on industry, asked the National Council of Social
Service to organize a tour for him to visit the black spots. It was a non-
stop tour. He heard hard-luck stories at first hand of men out of work.
He saw the dole queues. The ragged children. The empty shopping-
baskets. The grass growing between the paving stones. Hollow cheeks
of grey-faced men. Some were blunt and bitter. Downright rude. He
understood.

"I'd probably say a lot more if I was in their place," he said. "Why
should they pretend to be contented when they are hard-up, hungry,
and out of a job?"

The Duchess went on many trips with him. She saw poverty in the
raw—not for the first time. Endless miles of travelling. Interminable
hand-shakings. Speeches and prize-givings. Hospital presentations and
addresses of welcome. Mayors, aldermen, M.P.s, housewives, out-of-
works, and a hundred other sorts of humanity.

She was invariably sympathetic, sincerely interested, cheerful and
courteous. Her sincerity encouraged them. She was genuine. That was
what they liked.

What pleased people particularly was the warm, personal touch
which she brought to the most aridly dignified and conventional
affairs. They went up to Merseyside. The local bigwigs planned a
terrific programme of dinners and receptions. The Duke and Duchess
quietly suggested cutting some of them out so that they could give a
purely personal informal tea for the widows and relations of the sailors
who had perished when the submarine *Thetis* sank. They gave it in a

private room at Liverpool Airport. To this day women remember how the Duchess was almost in tears when she heard their stories, how the Duke played with the children and mended a toy motor-car for a tiny boy.

Another day they arrived at a children's home. The Committee were not there to meet them. The matron was horror-struck. "Never mind, we'll go and play with the children," the Duchess said. When the Committee turned up a few minutes later they found the Duchess rocking a wooden horse for a tiny girl whilst the Duke was on his knees playing trains with small children.

Meanwhile, Belgrave Square had become merely their London residence. Princess Victoria, a daughter of Edward VII, and the Duke's aunt, realized only too well that the young couple needed a house of their own.

So she left them Coppins, her own house at Iver, among the Buckinghamshire beech woods. Coppins is neither great, old, grand nor particularly beautiful. It is solid. It is homely. It sits in pleasant country but it epitomizes Victorianism in its least imaginative phase. A blend of Swiss Cottage and plain, unvarnished villadom. The bay windows, stone mullions, and transoms typify Victorian broadcloth and whiskers.

It was stuffed with furniture, overcrowded with pictures, decorated in dark colours. Almost, one expected antimacassars and aspidistras. None the less, it was a house—their very own.

The gardens were overshadowed by trees, darkened by laurels, prickly with holly. A kindly legacy but, none the less, a challenge.

Two young minds, each acutely conscious of beauty, took up the challenge. They did not destroy. They did not revolutionize. They improved. They let in the light.

Fussiness gave place to elegance. Overcrowded rooms became spacious. Redecoration, lighter colours, gay chintzes, welcomed the sun.

They hung their own pictures. Two or three superb flower pieces by that master of Dutch painting, van Huysum; an Anthony Devis; the family portraits by Laszlo, and two portraits of themselves by Sorine, a Russian painter who deserves to be better known.

Nothing short of an architectural face-lift could have altered the exterior but new paint worked wonders. It lightened and brightened the whole look of the house. Stolidity was banished.

In all this the Duke took a strong, personal lead.

"He had very definite ideas about furniture, and decoration, which he had inherited from his mother, Queen Mary," I was told by one who was very closely associated with the Duke and Duchess for years. "He practically ran the house and dictated its decoration. She was entirely dominated by him—and adored him. He collected very lovely furniture and he filled Coppins with chintzes and lightened its atmosphere inside and out.

"He also bought a great deal of exquisite furniture for a much larger house which he hoped to get later on, but it never came off. After the war the Duchess sent the surplus furniture to Christie's and had a very good sale.

"Then he re-organized the gardens. He spent hours cutting down laurels himself and letting in the sunlight, and did a lot of weeding. He loved doing odd jobs in the garden but the Duchess was not really keen on gardening, although she adored flowers. She likes beauty and grace of form in everything and detests ugliness—especially when it is disguised as 'functionalism'."

Among flowers the Duchess likes freesias for indoors and roses outdoors. One enters the rose garden at Coppins through gilt wrought-iron gates. They open on to the pergola, with Dorothy Perkins and American pillar roses cascading in a tumult of colour. The splendour of the roses is offset by misty-blue ranks of tall delphiniums. Roses, daffodils and the great magnolia grandiflora outside the drawing-room window are the dominant flower notes.

Princess Victoria placed a marble bust of her father, Edward VII, in the entrance hall, where it stands today. Beside it she kept a pot of the incense plant whose haunting scent greeted every visitor to the house.

The kitchens were thoroughly modernized but a portrait of Queen Victoria in a black and gilt frame still dominates the housekeeper's room.

Meals at Coppins were, and still are, often served in the heat of summer on a white painted table of wrought iron with a glass top. Under the glass, trays filled with roses, fuchsias, hydrangeas and other blooms which glow through the glass and give an impression of dining on a bed of flowers.

Today the house still contains many of the Duke's art treasures, including jewelled and enamelled boxes and small *objets d'art* by the Imperial Russian jeweller, Fabergé; some very good Chippendale furniture and a lot of Sèvres and Spode china.

The Duchess's jewels, most of which were chosen for her by the Duke, include a superb set of sapphires and diamonds given to her by Queen Mary, some magnificent tiaras, one of which was given by the City of London on her marriage, and an enchanting leaf spray of diamonds with a set of ear-rings and brooches which the Duke gave her on either the children's birthdays or on their own anniversaries. One of her favourite family heirlooms is a diamond bow brooch given to her by Princess Nicholas on her marriage to the Duke. She is particularly fond of sapphires, which are reputed to inspire the owner to good works. Her engagement ring is a sapphire.

As the children grew older, life at Coppins became, naturally, infinitely more attractive to them than life in London. They had their own sand-pit to play in, a see-saw, a slide and an outdoor gymnasium with ladders and swings, whilst the Home Farm with its cows, pigs, chickens and ducks, and Mouff, the Duke's Chow, were endlessly diverting animal friends. The Duke's Alsatian, Doushka, died aged fourteen in 1939.

At night the Duke played on his baby grand Ibeck piano, which he loved, whilst relatives and guests played backgammon or cards. There was a Steinway grand as well but he preferred the smaller one which he had owned before he was married. Although he loved a good deal of modern music and had a wonderful collection of jazz records, the Duke also played the classics, Beethoven's Symphonies, Brahms and Mozart.

Life in those days was young, fresh, gay and relatively carefree. They both fulfilled an enormous number of public engagements, often putting in a day's work which began at 9 a.m. and finished with a public function as late as 11 p.m., but they still made time for reading, music, painting, the theatre, gardening and the children.

Their tastes in books were wide. The Duke liked novels. The Duchess, as a close friend of hers remarked to me the other day, "still reads tremendously. Biographies, novels, books on art, memoirs and the rest. It is a great part of her life."

Coppins, as I remarked earlier, is not over-large. Apart from the dining-room there are two sitting-rooms, a music room, about six bedrooms and a nursery. It was run comfortably, but not extravagantly, with a staff of six—a butler, footman, cook, housemaid, a daily maid or two, and two chauffeurs, most of whose time was then taken up with driving the Duke and Duchess on official business.

Looking through the memoirs of relations, listening to close friends, one gets the picture of a happy, utterly devoted couple, leading a packed and busy life, yet completely domesticated.

Little things paint the picture. He liked flying. She did not. Yet she always flew with him because it suited him to get there quicker. When she landed she remarked wryly: "It was pretty awful but it's all over —until we fly back."

He adored driving fast cars. She loved being driven by him. But she has never learnt to drive a car because she is not mechanically minded.

His favourite cocktail was gin and pineapple juice with a dash of lemon. She never drank cocktails but she smoked her favourite Greek cigarettes whilst he played the piano. Trivial if you like but revealing. The nuances of life.

Both possessed the almost lost art of good conversation. They could talk on art, politics, books, pictures, music or merely lighthearted nonsense. They missed nothing and enjoyed everything.

"What do you do at Coppins every week-end?" someone once asked her.

"We spend most of the time in the garden playing with the children," the Duchess answered gaily. The perfect week-end.

The truth is that during those five years between her marriage and the outbreak of war, the Duchess of Kent, quite unconsciously, *civilized* London. It needed it badly. The old standards of manners and behaviour had largely vanished. The old values were laughed at by the younger generation. The aftermath of the 1914–18 War saw to that.

The era needed a leader—an example. Royalty alone could give it. For Royalty, in this modern world, still has that indefinable something which not all the millions of the newest millionaires can ever produce.

The Duchess had that something. The Greeks have a word for it. "Porphyrogennitos"—the Descendant of Kings. But she had more than the blood of a thousand years. She had, as Kipling said, of the Thousandth Man, "the common touch". Her own two bitter periods of exile; the common-sense upbringing by her parents; her English nanny—all had taught her simple values, good manners and the worth of a devoted home-life. Added to it was her instinctive love of beauty.

All this she translated, quite unconsciously, into a shining example for the youth of the period. She brought new and essentially good standards of taste in clothes, hats, decoration, furnishings and above

Surrounded by a group of Dyak warriors, the Duchess poses on the lawn of the
Residency at Sibu, Sarawak, during her Far East tour, 1952

Canada, 1954. The Duchess pressed the button to start a new generator at
Niagara Falls

The Duchess being greeted by Dr. Kwame Nkrumah, when she arrived in Accra for the Ghana independence celebrations in 1957

A rodeo was provided as entertainment when the Duchess and Princess Alexandra visited Mexico City in 1959 on their tour of Central and South America

all, manners and behaviour, to a world which badly needed them. She dressed well. The rest followed. The *outré* died in consequence. Designers had to think again. Thereby women's clothing, and particularly their hats, improved out of all recognition.

She had natural good manners herself and would not tolerate bad manners in others. The "casualness" which had become the everyday badge of far too many people's behaviour, received a jolt.

Above all, she was domesticated. So domesticity, that outmoded Victorianism, became popular again.

Thus the Duchess, without consciously realizing it, did England a lot of good when we needed it. She epitomized decent standards. Most English women saw in her the qualities they admired. She was feminine, artistic, domestic, decisive in her likes and dislikes, a good wife, a wonderful mother. All those values were in danger in that age of cocktail values.

So you have the picture of a hard-working, devoted, gaily artistic young couple, carrying the burden of Royalty with charm and dignity but with little of its state, splendour or revenues.

It could have gone on, usefully, youthfully. But already across the Channel, the marching feet, the glitter of bayonets, the roll of drums, the rattle of tanks, told that the lights were going out again in Europe. Tragedy was on the march.

Their joint success in public life was so great, their popularity so soundly founded that when the Duke visited Poland many influential Poles begged him to accept the Crown of Poland. An English King on the old throne of the Sobieskis was, in their eyes, the best guarantee of a safe future. The Duke of Kent and his Duchess not only looked the part but could have played it to the manner born.

It was not their only success on the Continent. In all their European travels they were first-class ambassadors for Britain. The Duke was appointed Governor-General of Australia in 1938. Australians were delighted. The women especially looked forward to greeting the Duchess as the natural leader of fashion and values. They were due to arrive in November, 1939.

So they chose their furniture, shipped it to Government House— where Princess Alexandra saw some of it in 1959 when she stayed there as the guest of Field Marshal Lord Slim.

Then on Sunday, September 3rd, the Duchess sat in the sunny sitting-room at Coppins listening to the radio.

"We are at war with Germany."

8

For the third time in her life war was to hit hard and bitterly at her house and family.

CHAPTER TEN

War, Bombs and the Duke's Death

THE WAR struck hard and deep at the roots of the Duchess's family life. One sister, Princess Elizabeth, was married to Count Toerring and in Germany. Her other sister, Princess Olga, was in Yugoslavia with the Regent, Prince Paul, her husband. Her mother, Princess Nicholas of Greece, was alone in her palace in Athens, still in mourning for the Duchess's father, Prince Nicholas. He had gone back when the Greek monarchy was restored and there died in February, 1938.

Thus, at a stroke, the Duchess was cut off from the two sisters, inseparable since childhood, and the mother whom they all adored.

Wherever they had been the three daughters had telephoned their parents almost every evening of their lives. They and their three husbands had constantly visited each other. No Royal family was more devoted and closely knit. War sliced those bonds like a knife.

To make matters worse, her aunt, Princess Andrew, mother of the Duke of Edinburgh, was also in Greece, beset by troubles. For although her son, Philip, was in the British Navy, her three daughters were married to German officers. She and Princess Nicholas stayed in Athens through all the horrors which followed. They gave themselves, heart and soul, to Red Cross work, and, through endless hardships, lived only for news of their children.

Here in England, in comparative safety, the Duchess of Kent heard from time to time of the hardships her mother was suffering. Thus apart from the ordinary family anxieties at home which she shared with every other Englishwoman the Duchess had the extra strain of worry concerning her relatives in Europe.

She threw herself heart and soul into war work. At the King's suggestion she became Commandant of the W.R.N.S. The Princess Royal was Commandant of the A.T.S. and the Duchess of Gloucester was Commandant of the W.A.A.F.

The Duke of Kent had already given up the lease at 3 Belgrave Square as he had expected to take his family to Australia on his appointment as Governor-General. That appointment was postponed. Instead he became a Rear-Admiral in the Navy for a short time and was then posted to the R.A.F. attached to the staff of the Inspector-General.

The late Dame Vera Laughton Mathews, then Director of the W.R.N.S., very kindly gave me first-hand impressions of the Duchess's service.

"She was," Dame Vera said, "kindness and charm itself, with a genuine interest in other people, a strong sense of duty and a sincere desire to help the Wrens. She has the most delightful speaking voice with a very faintly foreign accent.

"I remember quite well when she paid her first visit to our head-quarters in Charing Cross. She turned up looking very beautiful and extremely smart in her new uniform. But her collar was too low and her gloves were white! After all, she had never spent much of her life in uniform before.

"She took one look at the officers who were waiting with me to receive her, glanced at her hands and said:

" 'Oh, dear! My gloves are all wrong, and my collar's awful!'

"She burst out laughing and we all joined in. That broke the ice. From then on she was a friend and an inspiration to us all.

"She often carried a handbag when she inspected parades, which was not strictly according to regulations. On one occasion she handed her bag to the Superintendent. The latter, who wouldn't be seen dead with a handbag in uniform, passed it on to Lady Herbert, the Duchess's Lady-in-Waiting, saying:

" 'Here, this is your job.' "

"The Duchess's sense of duty was invincible. She never cut her programme, no matter how heavy it might be or how behind-time events might make her. Her view was that a lot of people had taken a lot of trouble to prepare things and she was not going to disappoint them no matter how late it made her. She started a tour of one Naval station at 9 a.m. one day and finished that night at a civic function in Glasgow at 11 p.m. No time even for half an hour's rest.

"I remember one charming incident at a big naval station when a young steward, who had been a factory-hand, waited on her during tea. Afterwards I asked the girl how she had enjoyed the occasion.

"Oh! How I wish me mother could 'ave seen me!" she exclaimed delightedly. "I'll bet she never thought I'd do anything like this."

Superintendent Man Currie, who also saw a good deal of the Duchess during her time with the W.R.N.S. remembers her visiting Dover College where the naval ratings had a basement dining-room. She sat down to tea with them whilst a raid was one, bombs dropping and anti-aircraft guns thundering. She talked cheerfully with everyone and did not seem to be in the least perturbed by the raid.

In conjunction with Dame Vera Laughton Mathews and Lord Alexander of Hillsborough, then First Lord of the Admiralty, the Duchess was responsible for the choice of the Wrens' hats. With her instinctive flair for dress she studied every design submitted with the utmost care and tried on some of the models herself.

"No woman wants to wear a hat which makes her look unattractive, war or no war," she said. "The right sort of hat is most important if we're to get recruits."

"The Duchess's own personal charm was one of our greatest aids in recruiting," Dame Vera Laughton Mathews told me. "Every time a photograph of her in Wren uniform appeared in the Press, girls rushed to join up. When she broadcast for recruits, the response was enormous. Whenever she went on a tour of inspection she insisted on seeing the girls' quarters, the galleys, the cooks, the menus and everything that conduced to their comfort. She was indefatigable.

"She always took the keenest interest in the personal side of the ratings' lives. When she was touring a station the girls would be standing by their beds. Usually the Duchess would pick up photographs belonging to them and ask them if it was their boy friend or a relative and if so what he was doing. This was not just make-weight conversation. She was really sincerely interested in the welfare of the women in the Service. And the women were quick to recognize that fact."

Apart from her official duties with the W.R.N.S. the Duchess served as a hospital nurse. She began by working at the Cottage Hospital at Iver making swabs and bandages. When she had mastered the elementary routine she "enlisted" as an auxiliary nurse under the name of Nurse Kay at University College Hospital in London. There she worked for weeks without anyone, other than the senior staff, being aware of her identity.

Miss J. M. Bond, now Assistant Matron at St. Pancras Hospital, then a sister at U.C.H., has many memories of Nurse Kay.

"She did all the ordinary jobs," she told me. "Mrs. Jackson, who was then the Matron, sent for me one day and told me that the Duchess of Kent was to work on my ward (No. 16) as an auxiliary. She was to be known as Nurse Kay and her identity was to be a close secret. The Registrar and Senior Surgeon obviously knew what was afoot but the news didn't leak out for the first few weeks.

"The Duchess was escorted up to the ward on the first day by the

Matron. She was neat and smart in a plain, well-cut, white coat. Not the ordinary uniform—blue coats—as worn by the auxiliaries, nor the striped dress and white apron worn by student nurses.

"The Duchess came and went much as she liked—or as official commitments would permit. She took part in all routine activities in the ward—surgical dressings, bedmaking, washing patients, doing hair, tidying lockers, plumping up pillows, feeding and handing round meals on trays. She assisted in the pre-operative preparation of patients who were due for the theatre but I don't remember her attending an operation. She saw them on to the table and the removal of tubes after the operation was also part of her job.

"She neither slept nor fed at the hospital. She was very friendly with the Matron—Mrs. Jackson—a woman of immense charm, very efficient, extremely likeable and quite unlike the dragon-like caricature of the usual matron. They became firm friends and were entirely at ease in each other's company. The Duchess would have coffee with the Matron before going up to the ward.

"The Hospital was in a very vulnerable position. It is built in the shape of a cross, and each ward has the same construction. This is to give more light and space. Therefore there was an unusual amount of glass to cause accidents from blast.

"The Duchess never visited a shelter during her spell at U.C.H. Nobody bothered much about sheltering as we were all too busy! She nursed lots of bomb victims as most of the inmates of the ward were emergency cases. The ward was extremely busy and the 'turn-over' very quick as we were desperately short of staff.

"Her personality as a nurse was very charming. She was very willing and worked hard. If she was ever without a concrete job she would always find something to do, such as tidying a patient's locker, talking to her, making tea or finding newspapers.

"One day a Registrar visited a patient in the ward. At luncheon that day he remarked: 'One of the V.A.D.s in No. 16 looks the spit image of the Duchess of Kent!'

" 'How extraordinary,' remarked our Senior Registrar, who, of course, knew all about it. 'What a coincidence.'

"It was two weeks later before the other Registrar realized that the V.A.D. was in fact the Duchess.

"The news leaked out bit by bit but because of my position as Sister-in-Charge of the ward, I would naturally be the last to hear any gossip which may have been going round the hospital.

"I didn't always know when the Duchess was coming on duty. One day the Matron telephoned me to say that they were on their way up. I groaned! She asked why. I said I had been up most of the night and had given my staff nurse half a day off. I was hoping to catch up on a bit of sleep between 10 a.m. and midday. 'But I suppose I shan't be able to now!'

"When the Duchess arrived she took one look at me and said: 'How tired you look! Please don't stay.'

" 'That certainly wasn't included in your training, Matron Bond,' I said. 'To be turned out of your own ward—by a nurse!'

" 'Ah! Well!' she laughed, 'I took it as a Royal Command, you know. And I was jolly glad to get it! I had a good sleep and the next morning the Duchess remarked that I looked much less tired and she hoped I felt better. She missed nothing.'

"My general impression of the Duchess during the time that she was with us was that she was genuinely interested in the care of the sick, more than in the medical aspect of medicine itself. She was a most pleasant person to have on the ward. Always amenable, adaptable, no trouble whatever and more than anxious to do all she could to help in every way."

The late Mrs. Jackson, who was Matron at University College Hospital, once said that after a raid in which a Servicemen's Hostel received a direct hit, a lot of badly wounded Canadian and Australian troops were brought in. Most were badly burnt and some had little time to live. The Duchess was just about to go off duty when the casualties came in.

"I can't possibly leave now, Matron," she said, catching Mrs. Jackson by the arm. "Is there anything I can do?"

"I'm afraid there's not much we can do for many of them," the Matron answered, "but, if you like, you can give them great pleasure. Most of them are overseas men, far from their own people. Why not take off your uniform, put on your outdoor clothes and go in and see them, not as a nurse but as a member of the Royal family. It'll do them a world of good. Tell them you came because you heard about them. It'll be perfectly true."

The Duchess changed out of uniform and went down to the casualty department where she stayed for more than an hour talking with the wounded men and cheering them up.

The one slightly comic moment during those bleak days of pain and daily death was when the Duke of Kent, as President of the Hospital, made an official visit. The Duchess went to the Sister of her ward one morning in dismay.

"I've just heard my husband is here making an official visit. Don't you think I'd better slip out quickly. If the patients see us together I'm afraid they'll guess."

"They'll guess it much more quickly if you rush away," the Sister replied. "You'd better stay and bluff it out."

A few seconds later the Duke walked into the ward. Nurse Kay was presented with the rest of the nurses and gave him the most polished curtsey. He acknowledged it without the flicker of an eyelid!

Then the Matron and Sister conducted him round the ward with the Duchess following well in the rear as an obscure nurse.

The Duke turned up one day when a heavy raid was going on. London shuddered to bombs and gunfire. Bloodstained stretchers, full of wounded, were being carried into the casualty reception department. The Duke went down to see if he could help.

"I might be able to give a hand with the stretchers anyway," he said.

A little boy, about as old as his own son, lay crying in a corner, sobbing for his father. The Duke went over to the child, patted him on the shoulder and took his hand.

"It's all right, old chap," he said kindly. "Your daddy will be here soon but I'm going to stay with you for a bit." He told the sobbing child an adventure story. In a few minutes the sobs ceased. The boy was sitting up, bright-eyed with interest.

The Duchess's secret was discovered in the end by a dressmaker's assistant. This girl, who read all the fashion papers, came into her ward as a patient. Nurse Kay brought her dinner. The patient could not take her eyes off her.

"You must tell me," she said to the Sister. "Isn't that V.A.D. the Duchess of Kent?"

The Sister smiled.

"People are always asking us that," she said, "it's Nurse Kay."

The new patient sniffed. She was not convinced. She followed Nurse Kay with her eyes whenever she came into the ward during the rest of the day. Then she announced:

"That V.A.D. *is* the Duchess of Kent. I've seen her picture dozens of times. Nobody is going to tell me it isn't her."

The secret was out.

Apart from her hospital work and her duties with the W.R.N.S. the Duchess visited endless factories, making anything from tanks to toothpaste; emergency hospitals; rest centres; bombed areas; fire stations and A.R.P. depots. She averaged 300 miles a week and her working day often began at 7 a.m. and finished at midnight.

As for the Duke, he flew over 60,000 miles in 12 months, to R.A.F. stations in Britain and overseas, in addition to visiting the President of Portugal and inspecting dozens of aircraft factories, shipyards and blitzed areas.

He overworked himself to the bone. So did the Duchess. In addition to her official work she ran the household at Coppins with a reduced staff, coped with rations, planned the meals herself and saw to her children. Meanwhile, another baby was on the way by the end of 1941.

All this time she was in constant agony for her husband's safety. Many times he was in personal danger from bombs, machine-gun fire and shells. In July, 1940, visiting an air-base, he stayed in a house on the perimeter. Four minutes after he left the house a bomb dropped within a few yards, went up in a blast of flame and wrecked the place— death missed by minutes.

He went down to the East End dozens of times whilst raids were on and was in one shelter holding no less than 7,000 people whilst the place shuddered to bomb-blast.

Once a time-bomb blew up with a terrific explosion within yards of his car. Bricks, broken glass and debris rained down. The Duke stopped his car, got out, perfectly unperturbed, walked across to a group of people, and said:

"That was a near thing, wasn't it? I am very glad to see that none of you are hurt."

Mr. Emil Davies, who was Chairman of the London County Council at the time, recalls that in 1941 the Duke of Kent drove him for four hours through the London docks under a constant rain of bombs, anti-aircraft shells and machine-gun bullets. It was a really lively raid. Everything was going up and a great deal more was coming down.

"However, as the Duke appeared to be oblivious to it all I did my best to look equally indifferent," Mr. Davies remarked afterwards.

The truth was that the Duke had that cool, boyish courage typical of the best of young Englishmen.

"He never batted an eyelid under shellfire or up in the air," a close friend told me. "In fact, I think he rather enjoyed the fun and the risk of it all. The only thing that worried him was that he was a bad sailor but he couldn't help that because his stomach was constitutionally at variance with the sea. Sea-sickness was the plague of his life when he was in the Navy. But under fire he was as cool as a cucumber.

"His main thought was always for others—particularly children. He had a very soft spot for them. Children in the bombed areas absolutely wrung his heart. You could see that in his face."

He and the Duchess were in the first air raid of the war. That was when he was stationed at Rosyth as a Rear-Admiral, Staff Officer, Intelligence, on the staff of the C.-in-C., Admiral Sir C. G. Ramsey, K.C.B.

Nearby he rented a house called Pitliver Castle where the Duchess joined him. He refused to be parted from her for long.

The German raiders hit a cruiser and a destroyer and tried to get the Forth Bridge.

Thus the Duke and Duchess were in the forefront of the hazards of war from the first.

In the summer of 1941, the Duke flew the Atlantic in a Liberator, toured thousands of miles in Canada to report on the working of the Commonwealth Air Training Plan, dined in mess with the pilots of the R.A.F. Ferry Command in Montreal and then flew on to the U.S.A. to inspect aircraft factories.

There he addressed 13,000 workmen at one meeting. He was a shy speaker but that day he surpassed himself.

Instead of using the stiff, official speech prepared for him he talked simply and naturally as man-to-man about the war-time trials of the ordinary families in Britain. He told them what raids meant to the working-class family, how war-time homes were run, about the children of Britain—including his own—and then gave them a few telling word-pictures of the tragedies he had seen among bombed-out victims in hospital—including babies. That speech brought the realities of war home to the men who were making the aircraft which were to help win the Battle of Britain. It made those American workmen, many of them critics of Britain, realize that on their efforts depended the lives of thousands of innocent people, men, women and babies. They cheered him to the roof.

He spent a day or two with President and Mrs. Roosevelt at Hyde Park, their country place. When he saw a big dish of oranges and bananas he fell on them like a boy.

"I haven't seen one, let alone eaten one, for about a year," he said.

Mrs. Roosevelt gave him a box of oranges and bananas to take back to England for his children.

When the bomber which brought him back to England touched down at the airfield, the Duchess was waiting for him. A close friend has told me that she went through an unending agony of apprehension during those war years whilst the Duke was flying. It almost seemed as though she had a premonition of the tragedy to come.

He brought back with him a toy motor-car for Prince Edward's sixth birthday. They gave a tea party at Coppins to celebrate. His two little nieces, Princess Elizabeth and Princess Margaret, were there. They loved their youngest uncle. He chased them round the garden and knew exactly how to play with children and talk to them on their own level.

So, for the last few weeks of that fatal summer of 1942, they lived their life together. The baby was born at Coppins on July 4th, a beautiful boy, the image of his mother. "Dear Foxy", the Duchess's old nanny, came down from London especially for his birth. She was the last remaining link in England with the Duchess's own childhood. Her father was dead. Her mother was in Greece, now under the heel of the Germans. Her sister Elizabeth was in Bavaria, and her other sister, Olga, was in East Africa, for revolt had broken out in Yugoslavia and they had had to flee. The world was in ferment—the blackest days of the war. Germany was on the triumphant march.

The King was grey with worry. Day after day the Duke of Kent was in London conferring with the King, his Ministers, with Service chiefs. The skies were lit by night with the fantastic geometry of war. The questing beams of searchlights, the shivering staccato flashes of gunfire. The thud and blast of bombs.

Yet at Coppins the flowers were in full bloom. The trees loomed like green galleons against the high skies of summer. The sun shone, and the Duke's carnations, her own roses, were a blaze of colour.

They christened Prince Michael on August 4th at Windsor Castle. His father stood proxy for Franklin Roosevelt, his American godfather. A simple christening. Members of the Royal family, Lord and Lady Herbert, a few other close friends and the staff from Coppins. The servants mingled with the guests and the Duke presented each to the Queen. Then they all drank the baby's health.

Exactly three weeks after the baby's christening the Duke drove off from Coppins in his own car *en route* for Invergordon. There he was to start on a secret flight to Iceland—his last tour of inspection. There would have been no more. The pilot and co-pilot were picked especially for the job. He wore the uniform of an Air-Commodore for he had relinquished his rank of Air Vice-Marshal so that he should not be superior to more experienced officers with whom he had to work. That was typical.

The Duchess waved to him as the car went down the drive and he turned for a last farewell look.

That afternoon the great Sunderland flying-boat took off down the Cromarty Firth, climbed, and turned north for Iceland.

David Morison, an elderly Scottish crofter, and his son Hugh, were plodding through knee-high heather on a lonely hillside looking for stray sheep in the mist. They heard the engines of a great aircraft roaring towards them. It passed low overhead in a torrent of sound. An unseen monster of war in the quivering mist on that houseless mountain in the lonely north.

Then a thunderous crash, a vivid orange sheet of flame through the grey dusk. And silence.

Young Hugh Morison ran down the hillside to the rutted, stony road. His motor-cycle was propped against a rock. He jumped on it and roared off through the plover-haunted mist to call neighbours from lonely cottages and the police from the village in the Strath. They hunted the hills all that afternoon until night came down, black and voiceless. They found nothing.

They were out again at dawn, crofters, shepherds and police, with an old Highland doctor, seventy-one years of age, marching with them.

Just after midday, at one o'clock, they saw a whorl of blue smoke spiralling up from the mountain-side. The buckled fuselage, the shattered wings of a great Sunderland flying-boat. And in the heather, flung clear of the wreckage, were bodies. The doctor identified one by the wristlet on one arm. It was the Duke of Kent.

A few hours later a flight-sergeant, Andrew Jack of Grangemouth, Stirlingshire, staggered to the door of a lonely cottage six miles from the wreckage. He was bare-footed, without trousers, soaked to the skin, pale with exhaustion, half-dazed. The one survivor.

Flight-Sergeant Jack was thrown clear when the aircraft first hit a rock on the mountainside. It glanced off, turned over and crashed. Somehow, dazed and half stunned, he dragged bodies clear of the wreckage.

Then, stripped of his shoes and trousers when he was flung out of the aircraft, he stumbled all night through the heather, falling, rising, falling again.

The news was telephoned to Coppins that night. Miss Fox, the devoted old nanny who had lived through every crisis in the Duchess's life from her childhood upwards—and been her comforter—answered the telephone. Stunned, she stumbled upstairs. The Duchess was in bed. She heard those pathetic, faltering footsteps, the old hands fumbling at her bedroom door. And she knew what had happened before a word was spoken. It was the end of an idyll—the crushing, crowning tragedy in a young life already schooled too often in sadness.

In another room a seven-weeks-old baby slept peacefully.

The funeral service in St. George's Chapel, Windsor Castle, was simple, unforgettable. A circlet of garden flowers, a naked sword, symbols of the Duke of Kent's humanity and chivalry, remain in one's memory.

The Duchess had picked the flowers in a quiet corner of the garden at Coppins. They rested on the coffin beside the wreath from the King and Queen.

The sword, stark against the chancel wall, was the conquering blade of Edward III. Hanging like a cross behind the altar it stood for the ideals of chivalry enshrined in the chapel's foundations, tragically fulfilled in the manner of the Duke's death.

Five monarchs were there—King George VI, King Haakon of Norway, King George II of the Hellenes, King Peter of Yugoslavia, and Queen Wilhelmina of the Netherlands.

Near them stood the Duke's private chauffeur, Frederick Field, who had driven him nearly 400,000 miles in thirteen years, and Mrs. Bill, his old "nanny". They were not forgotten in a ceremony so intimate that not one Cabinet Minister, not even Mr. Churchill, was present. The Duke would have been glad that Mr. Field and Mrs. Bill were there to say good-bye to a friend.

Inspector James Evans, the Duke's personal detective, was there too, beside the Kings and Presidents. He had been with the Duke wherever he went except once. That was on the Duke's last flight. At the eleventh hour it was decided that he should not go.

As the procession entered the chapel three figures stood motionless in the south choir stalls. In the centre, the Duchess, on either side of her the Queen and Queen Mary. All were in deep mourning, their faces heavily veiled.

The Queen looked after her sister-in-law with firm sympathy. When, as they entered the choir stalls, the Duchess stumbled, and again when she appeared to be overcome, the Queen grasped her arm and laid a gloved hand on her waist.

The Duchess knelt in prayer as six N.C.O.s from R.A.F. fighter squadrons lowered the coffin on the catafalque. At the close of the service she paused to look down on the Duke's gold-braided Royal Air Force cap which lay on the coffin beside two crimson carnations, his favourite buttonhole.

The funeral procession was impressive in its simplicity. Only members of the Duke's family and his personal friends took part. It was headed by the Dean of Windsor, Dr. Baillie.

The coffin was preceded by the Lord Chamberlain, the Earl of Clarendon, by Lieut.-Colonel Humphrey Butler, and Captain Lord Herbert, equerries to the Duke of Kent, bearing the Duke's insignia on crimson cushions.

The pall bearers were Air Vice-Marshal F. H. McNamara, V.C., Air Vice-Marshal A. C. Maund and Air Marshal T. L. Leigh-Mallory on one side, and Air Vice-Marshal R. Graham, Air Vice-Marshal G. R. M. Reid and Air Marshal H. Edwards on the other.

Behind them came Garter King-of-Arms, Sir Gerald Wollaston, who proclaimed the Duke's styles and titles at the end of the service.

The King, in Royal Air Force uniform, headed the mourners. The Duke of Gloucester, in the khaki uniform of a lieutenant-general, was on his right, and Admiral Sir Lionel Halsey, representing the Duke of Windsor, on his left.

The service, conducted by the Dean, was painfully expressive of the delicate spirit of the man they mourned. It was reflected in the Duchess's choice of music for the organ. The Funeral March of Chopin was the one he had always admired while the Intermezzo No. 1 by Christian Sinding, the Scandinavian composer, was his favourite piece.

They were played by Dr. Harris, organist of St. George's Chapel. The Chapel choir sang the hymns.

As the Dean intoned the words, "Earth to earth, ashes to ashes," the King stepped forward to sprinkle a handful of earth over the coffin. Tears were in the King's eyes when he stepped back after this farewell to his young brother.

Trumpeters of the Royal Air Force sounded the Last Post and Reveille and the service was over. The Queen held the Duchess's hand as they moved slowly out of the chapel.

The dead Duke was only thirty-nine.

There was, of course, a memorial service in London—a moment of sad splendour and solemn prayer amid the daily clatter of war.

Perhaps the most human and certainly the most typically Cockney sidelight on that service was when two middle-aged London flower-girls, Mrs. Kate Farmiloe and Mrs. Mary McCarthy, left their pitches outside King's Cross Station and hailed a taxi-cab. They carried a great bunch of pink and red carnations with a centre of pink roses.

"Buckingham Palace, mate," they told the taxi-driver, "back door for us girls. This wreath is for the poor young Duke of Kent—from all the London flower-girls. He once bought a dozen red carnations and a bunch of white heather from Kate here. A proper gentleman he was."

That wreath of carnations and roses had its place of honour at the service.

In the House of Commons, Winston Churchill paid the tribute of all men in noble language.

"The loss of this gallant and handsome Prince in the prime of his life has been a shock to all the people of the British Empire. . . . I knew the late Duke of Kent . . . his overpowering desire was to render useful service to his King and Country in this period when we are all of us on trial.

"The Duke of Kent was ready to waive his rank, to put aside all ceremony, to undergo any amount of discomfort and danger in order to feel that he was making a real contribution to our national struggle for life and honour. . . ."

He went on, with rare understanding:

"There is something about death on active service which makes it different from common or ordinary death in the normal course.

"It is accepted without question by the fighting men. Those they leave behind them are also conscious of a light of sacrifice and honour which plays around the grave or the tomb of the warrior.

"They are, for the time being, uplifted.

"This adds to their fortitude but it does not in any way lessen their pain.

"Nothing can fill the awful gap, nothing assuage or comfort the loneliness and deprivation which fall on the wife and children when the prop and centre of their home is suddenly snatched away.

"Only faith in a life after death, in a brighter world where dear ones will meet again—only that and the measured tramp of time can give consolation.

"The Duke of Kent had a joyous union and a happy family . . . and I say, without hesitation, that all our thoughts go out in sympathy to H.R.H. The Duchess of Kent, the beautiful and stricken Princess, who, in her turn, tastes the bitter tribulation which war brings to so many."

In due course the Air Ministry held an official inquiry into the causes of the fatal accident. It was rumoured that a spy or enemy action had been to blame. Nothing was farther from the truth. Sir Archibald Sinclair, Secretary of State for War, said in the House of Commons:

"The aircraft, which was proceeding from a Royal Air Force station in Scotland to Iceland, was airborne just after one o'clock in the afternoon of August 25th. Before departure, the correct procedure for briefing the captain as to the exact route to be followed and for providing full information about the weather conditions likely to be encountered, was complied with. Local weather conditions were not good at the time of the take-off, but the general indications showed a likelihood of improvement to the westward.

"The captain of the aircraft was a flying-boat pilot of long experience on the particular type of aircraft which he was flying that day, and of exceptional ability.

"About half an hour after take-off the aircraft was heard approaching land from the sea at what appeared to be a low height, and shortly afterwards it was heard to crash into the hills.

"The Court found: First, that the accident occurred because the aircraft was flown on a track other than that indicated in the flight plan given to the pilot, and at too low an altitude to clear the rising ground on the track.

"Secondly, that the responsibility for this serious mistake in airmanship lies with the captain of the aircraft.

"Thirdly, that the weather encountered should have presented no difficulties to an experienced pilot.

"Fourthly, that the examination of the propellers showed that the engines were under power when the aircraft struck the ground."

(*Above*) Princess Alexandra patting a koala bear during her visit to Brisbane in 1959 for the Queensland centenary celebrations

(*Right*) An Australian win at Wimbledon—the Duke of Edinburgh, in company with the Duchess of Kent, a lifelong tennis fan, presenting the men's singles trophy to Neale Fraser

Welcome to President de Gaulle. The Duchess was at Gatwick Airport when
President and Mme de Gaulle arrived for a state visit

Danny Blanchflower introducing the Tottenham Hotspur team to the Duchess
before defeating Leicester City in the Cup Final, 1961

CHAPTER ELEVEN

The Aftermath

THE DUKE's death hit the Duchess a hammer-blow of grief. Twice exiled from her native Greece; her father gone; her mother and sisters in war-stricken countries—and now this.

"It changed her utterly almost overnight," I was told by a close friend of the Duchess, who was with her all through that dreadful period. "The Duke was a strong, forcible character, very like his father, King George V, in some ways. After his death the Duchess altered tremendously. She had been quite content to be guided and ruled by him.

"When she lost him she could have retired into semi-private life. Instead she determined to give the rest of her days to her children and to the duties which had been nearest to the Duke's own heart. She buried her sorrow in hard work. She seemed almost to become a new woman of character overnight—far more forceful, resolute and decided.

"Marry again? Oh no! I never thought she would want anyone to take the Duke's place and guide her life. Her children, her friends, her memories, her work—that's her life.

"She is devoted to her children. A very loyal friend to her friends. She is a tremendously warm, kind-hearted person with a catholic taste in people but she has few really close and intimate friends. Lots of acquaintances and lots of people she's glad to meet.

"She likes a diversity of people—musicians, artists, writers, some actors, almost anyone who has ability and a real feeling for beauty and good taste.

"She is extremely observant of people's manners and very exacting with her own children. She sees that they wait on her guests and behave with the utmost good manners.

"She has a low, attractive voice with a very faintly foreign accent on a word here and there, such as 'really', for example. But she thinks of herself—and *is* in all her ways and loyalties—as completely British. *This* is her country and no other.

"She is very fond of films and straight plays, but her sense of good taste is far too pronounced for her to tolerate trash or sordidness. She reads an enormous lot."

When the Duke died his Civil List of £25,000 a year ceased. His widow received nothing from Parliament. She was left in financial circumstances vastly different from those of her married life. She did not even draw the R.A.F. pension to which she was entitled.

Coppins, which the Duke once described to a friend of mine as "no more than a big cottage", became the ultimate home. Finances would not run to anything more ambitious. The bigger house on which they had set their hearts vanished—a dream into thin air.

So the Duchess sent much of the superb furniture, silver, china, and pictures which the Duke had collected with such care and discrimination, for that dream-house, to Christie's. It was a very good sale—high prices for vanished hopes.

Luckily, King George VI and Queen Mary came to her financial rescue. Her income was assured. Far from large but just enough. The "big cottage" was run on something very like a shoestring.

Meanwhile, she threw herself into an immense amount of public service—anything to forget. For a long time the Duke's name was scarcely mentioned. Tactful mayors and local dignitaries more than once deleted references to him from their intended speeches because it was realized by those nearest to the Duchess that any mention of her husband would cause unnecessary pain. She was, in truth, the tragic widow who nursed her grief and worked herself to the bone to forget it.

This tremendous burden of public work meant spending a lot of time in London.

The problem of accommodation was solved in 1954 when she was given a grace-and-favour apartment of some twenty-two rooms in Kensington Palace. About eight of those rooms are in constant daily use as offices with a busy staff of Ladies-in-Waiting, a Private Secretary, secretaries, and a telephone switchboard—a hive of activity as busy as any City office.

The King had already, years before, promised the Duke of Kent that he should have the apartment which his aunt, Princess Louise, Duchess of Argyll, had occupied for many years. After the Duke's death the King said to the Duchess:

"You shall have those rooms which I promised to the Duke."

During the war, however, Kensington Palace was bombed. A good deal of damage was done. Moreover, dry rot set in in some rooms.

The place badly needed renovating. So it was not until 1955 that the Duchess was able to move in.

Her rooms are high, light and have an air of eighteenth-century spaciousness. From the windows one sees a vista of broad lawns, splendid trees and massed shrubs—the parkland view of a great country house in London. Much of the palace, however, is still empty and awaiting repairs by the Ministry of Works.

She has a small walled garden of her own. And here is a charming story about it. Not long ago a mallard duck flew backwards and forwards past her window quacking loudly. On the lawn of the little walled garden waddled his mate with ten tiny ducklings paddling behind her. The walls are twelve feet high so the family was obviously imprisoned.

Her Comptroller and a policeman spent the next two hours catching the ducklings and transporting them tenderly to the Round Pond where they were joined by their frantic parents.

To return to the period immediately after the Duke's death. Despite her sorrow and the press of work the Duchess put her children and their upbringing first and foremost.

"She gave them a solid, sensible education," a close friend told me. "No extravagance, no nonsense and no false values. She is devoted but very firm."

Five years after the Duke's death she engaged Katherine Peebles, a delightful Scotswoman, full of charm and commonsense, to act as governess to Prince Michael. She was recommended by the Duke and Duchess of Gloucester and later became governess to Prince Charles and Princess Anne. Princess Alexandra immediately christened her "Bambi", after Walt Disney's endearing little deer, whilst the rest of the family generally referred to her as "Misspy" (short for Miss P.). She became a family friend.

The Duke of Kent, after some years at Ludgrove, a preparatory school near Wokingham, went to Eton in the September term of 1948. He was then thirteen years old. The following February, Princess Alexandra, eleven years old, became a boarder at Heathfield, near Ascot. The Duchess particularly asked that she should be given no special privileges so mistresses and girls alike called her "Alexandra", and she settled down quickly to the everyday run of school life, helping to clear the dining-room table and tidy up her own bedroom as well as her lessons.

She was not particularly brilliant at any subject but definitely above average in English, French, History, and Art, good at swimming and rounders, fair at tennis, and an accomplished horsewoman.

She had learnt to ride a pony when she went to a private day school in Iver at the age of seven, and she took part in several horse shows before going to Heathfield.

After four years and a bit at Heathfield, she flew with her mother to Paris on October 17th, 1953, and stayed six months with the family of the Comte de Paris, Pretender to the Throne of France. The Comte and his wife, and eleven children, lived in a fifteen-roomed mansion called Cœur Volant, "The Flying Heart", in charmingly wooded grounds at Louveciennes, just outside Paris.

There Princess Alexandra improved her piano playing under Marguerite Long and was driven every day to Paris to the finishing school of Mademoiselle Anita. There she learnt cooking, dressmaking, current events and an appreciation of the arts. With the Comte's family, which included the twenty-year-old Prince Henri, his eldest son, and the twenty-one-year-old Princess Isabelle, she was able to polish up her French.

She came home to England finally in April, 1954, a highly competent, well-mannered, sweet-natured young girl with a new confidence in life and well able to face the years of public duty ahead of her.

Lady Moyra Hamilton, twenty-four-year-old daughter of the Duke and Duchess of Abercorn, who had been a maid-of-honour to the Queen at the Coronation, was appointed as her first Lady-in-Waiting.

Since that day, eight years ago, Princess Alexandra has increasingly played her part in the public duties of the Royal family. Today she is the double of her mother in good looks, poise, charm and hard work.

Whilst "Bambi" was acting as governess to Prince Michael in those early childhood days the Duchess looked for a holiday tutor for the young Duke of Kent—someone who could guide him in the ways of the world and keep his nose down to a reasonable amount of work during his holidays from Eton.

She chose a tall, twenty-one-year-old young man with a mane of black hair with the romantic name of Giles St. Aubyn.

St. Aubyn, a son of Lord St. Levan who owns that fantastic castle, St. Michael's Mount, which hangs like Mahomet between sea and heaven, became not only the young Duke's tutor but his friend and inspiration. Between them, "Bambi" and Giles conquered the young Duke's occasional fits of impatience which he had inherited from his father, and the occasional stubbornnesses of Princess Alexandra and

Prince Michael, who have much the same temperament. Miss Peebles handled them all with supreme patience, tact, good humour, and Scots firmness. Moreover, she could teach. No governess was ever more trusted, respected and loved.

Giles St. Aubyn set a high personal standard of good manners, fun and downright hard work which completely won the young Duke's trust and respect. He crowned almost any argument with the final clinching remark, "Well, Giles says that's all right. If Giles says a thing is right it must be right."

It was a tribute to the Duchess's uncanny flair for picking the right people that, left with three children and no husband to guide them, she was able to put her finger unerringly on a young woman and a young man who both had an inborn flair for handling children and understanding their minds and reactions.

The eldest boy, "Eddie", had the same quick mind as his father, the same alert interest in up-to-date things, the same dashing spirit. All he needed was a man not too old, just sufficiently older than himself, whom he could copy, admire and never regard as being stiff or an old fogey. Giles St. Aubyn was the answer.

He brought out in Eddie all the courtesy and good manners which had been inherent in his father.

In his later young manhood the present Duke of Kent has been encouraged by his mother to be self-reliant without being foolhardy. He was not given a great deal of money to spend and his hobbies and holidays were of the simplest sort. When in Switzerland, for example, he stayed at a guest house of the most modest sort. No one could say that he had been brought up with a silver spoon in his mouth.

Today Princess Marina spends most of her working week at Kensington Palace. There, as a close friend told me: "The decorations are entirely her own choice and design. Some very lovely chintzes, particularly in the drawing-room. One of them is a rather grand room which she has translated into a very lived-in room with a friendly family atmosphere. Her china is exceptionally lovely. She has a lot of good Meissen and other fine Continental china and she is very proud in a quiet way of her lovely things.

"She has had all the bedrooms done in a country-house style of furnishing. Mainly eighteenth-century mahogany furniture, none of it very heavy in style.

"All official lunches and dinner parties are given at Kensington Palace rather than at Coppins, where she entertains personal friends on a very small scale. Small luncheon parties of perhaps eight or ten people, with two or three guests sometimes staying for the week-end. Never more.

"They dine at a long table and there is some very nice Georgian silver and silver-gilt plate with, usually, vases of mixed flowers."

As for the guests, they may be anyone from ambassadors and statesmen to people of very many different professions. The Duchess likes to keep in touch with all useful forms of modern thought and work. She is a very alive person.

Her vitality and sense of high duty were never better demonstrated than when on Saturday, September 27th, 1952, she flew from London Airport to Singapore on one of the longest, most arduous and valuable Royal tours undertaken since the war. The Duke of Kent, then sixteen, went with her.

It all began in a relatively small way. The Singapore Anti-Tuberculosis Association had built a new clinic. They wanted the Duchess, as President of the National Association for the Prevention of Tuberculosis, to open it. So the Government of Singapore invited her and she accepted.

That sparked off a train of suggestions. First, her own regiment, now known as the Queen's Own Buffs, of which she is Colonel-in-Chief, was serving in Malaya. The anti-terrorist warfare was at its height. Rubber plantations were being sabotaged by the Reds. Murder kept a daily date. Every soldier was a target. The Duchess decided to inspect her regiment, risks or no risks.

Then someone suggested that, as she had been war-time Commandant of the W.R.N.S., she might care to see the great Naval base at Singapore.

Malayan rajahs and tribal chieftains begged her to visit them. The Sultan of Brunei, the rulers of North Borneo, the Dyaks and headhunters of Sarawâk, the great and splendid city of Hong Kong, all clamoured to see her. Invitations flew in like swallows. They were accepted.

Thus began a momentous tour. For the first time since the war, a member of the British Royal family visited all the British territories in South-east Asia, Singapore, Malaya, Sarawâk, North Borneo, Hong Kong, and Brunei.

The Duchess flew out in the Argonaut airliner, *Atalanta*, in which the Queen, as Princess Elizabeth, had flown with the Duke of Edinburgh to East Africa, earlier in that year. With her went Lady Rache

Davidson as Lady-in-Waiting; Lord Althorp, a temporary Equerry; and Mr. Philip Hay, the Duchess's Private Secretary, and Comptroller.

They flew through the autumn skies, above the bright harvest fields of Britain, to Rome and the blue seas of Cyprus. There they stayed the night. Then on to Bahrein, high over the tawny Arabian desert; to Karachi, and so down the coast of India, to Colombo for a day. Three and a half days after leaving London they came, in the gold of early evening, over a gentle sea, to the sprawling splendour of Singapore—the white beaches, the opal seas and jungle backcloth of the City of the Lion.

As the airliner touched down twenty-five-pounder guns of the Royal Artillery thundered a twenty-one-gun salute to greet the first Royal visitor for nearly a quarter of a century.

The door of the aircraft opened. Out stepped the Duchess, coolly elegant in a gold silk dress, full-skirted, and a gold pill-box hat. She carried a small black fan in her left hand. The perfect touch—the one concession to a blazing sky.

A murmur of admiration rustled through the crowds waiting there in the shimmering heat. That air of regal informality, peculiarly her own, made an unforgettable, instant impression.

It was easy to see that Singapore was in the war zone. Hundreds of uniformed and plain-clothes police and Servicemen guarded the airport and the route to Government House. Tens of thousands of natives had swarmed into the city to meet her. Chinese, Indians, Malays, hill-tribesmen, little men from the jungle, British rubber planters, Europeans—they were all there. Any man of that brown and yellow maelstrom could be a terrorist, itching to take a shot at the Royal visitors.

The Duchess knew that. Never by sign or word did she betray the slightest fear or apprehension.

Two thousand cheering, flag-waving children of all colours and races shrilled their welcome. It was typical of that entire tour that, wherever she went, the Duchess was greeted by swarms of children and by Asiatics of all races. Whites, yellows and intermediate colours mixed with perfect freedom. It was a Royal tour with a difference—the V.I.P.s wisely let the Duchess see, and be seen by, the people.

More than once, in the days that followed, she walked into shops on her own to buy things. Once it was a loaf of bread. Another day she spent more than an hour trying on Chinese slippers and jackets. She bought a lot of them as Christmas presents for the Royal family and for friends at home. Any of those informal visits could have ended in assassination. Too many of her family had died thus in Europe. She took the risk.

There were plenty of formal occasions—no less than sixty-five visits and receptions of pomp and State at which people saw a regal, gracious woman who epitomized the humanity and dignity of the British Throne.

Equally, they saw the friendly, charming side of her, her eager interest in children, cripples, the wounded and the very poor. One or two shopkeepers even found out that it was bad business to try to overcharge the Royal visitor. She went elsewhere!

This gives an idea of the sheer hard work packed into a few days. On October 2nd she inspected the Singapore Naval base, one of the largest in the world. The temperature was 95° F. in the shade! You could have fried an egg on a battleship's deck.

Next day she opened the tuberculosis clinic, able to take 5,000 patients a day; then she visited barracks. Next she walked endless miles round hospitals—a cheerful word for patients in every ward. That night she appeared, cool, radiant and gracious, at a ball at Government House. She danced until the small hours.

Next morning she inspected the giant R.A.F. station at Changi. All this meant miles of walking in tropic heat. Flies, dust, hundreds of handshakes. The right word in the right place to the right person. Always a ready smile, quick sympathy and alert interest. She missed nothing and no one.

Yet the following morning, October 5th, instead of taking a day off in that sweltering heat, the Royal aircraft roared into the air. The Duchess and her party were on their way to Kuala Lumpur, capital of the Federation of Malaya, 250 miles away. Below them lay mountains, jungles, hills and rivers. There the bandit war was in full swing. Men prowled with murder in their hearts.

At Kuala Lumpur, the High Commissioner, General Sir Gerald Templer, made elaborate precautions for the safety of the Royal party. A bullet-proof armoured car awaited the Duchess. A convoy of armoured cars was drawn up behind it. R.A.F. bombers and fighters droned overhead. Troops were everywhere. She was in the heart of the fighting zone.

The Duchess stayed in King's House, as Sir Gerald and Lady Templer's guest, whilst the Duke stayed in another mansion called Carcosa, as the guest of the Deputy High Commissioner, Sir Donald

McGillivray. Both houses, set high on twin mountain peaks in the
lovely Lake Gardens of Kuala Lumpur, were guarded by double
relays of sentries.

Out in the jungle and along the roads which the Duchess had yet to
travel, came the distant thump of bombs. The R.A.F. were strafing
the roadside jungles to put bandits on the run. It was just as well they
did. A machine-gun ambush had been constructed which would have
swept her convoy with murderous fire.

That first afternoon the Duchess was due to inspect a thousand
members of the defence, welfare, health and youth organizations of
the city. The population of Kuala Lumpur had planned otherwise.

When the Raja Muda, or Crown Prince, of Selangor, walked with
her on to the parade ground and received the Royal salute, he opened,
as it were, a pageant of absolutely blinding colour.

He, the Raja Muda, was dressed in bright silken robes with a splendid head-dress. In his sarong he carried a gold-handled kris, or Malayan
dagger. A servant marched behind holding a bright yellow umbrella
over his head.

There to greet the Duchess were men and women of almost every
race under the Eastern sun—Chinese, Tamils, Malays, Punjabi Mussul-
men, Chettiars and, shyly skulking, the little broad-lipped Sakai from
the mountains. Indian turbans, Malayan sarongs and the brilliant saris
of the women dazzled the hot sunlight.

The people had poured in from jungle and mountainside, from
towns and villages all over Malaya. Some came by special aircraft.
Others packed the trains and buses like flies. Hundreds came in croco-
dile processions on bicycles. Many more on foot. The words "racial
segregation" had never been heard.

Even the bands were of mingled races. Pipers of the Gordon High-
landers marched with Gurkha pipers from the Kingdom of Nepal.
Malayan police, in white and blue, played in step with men of the
Twelfth Lancers and the Manchester Regiment. The rolls of drums
and fifes, shrieking of bagpipes, shrill cheers from ten thousand throats.
An incredible, unforgettable day of *Arabian Nights* splendour.

Next day the Duchess and her son, still fresh and smiling, flew
100 miles over tiger-haunted hills and jungles to the ancient city of
Malacca, the glittering Oriental cradle of four great civilizations—
British, Dutch, Portuguese and Chinese.

There they were taught how to tap rubber from a rubber tree.
Then she was presented with an ivory-handled kris, the wavy-bladed

dagger of the Malay, by a Malayan prince, Dato Mohammed Shah. His great-great-grandfather fought against the British in 1881.

"Today," he said to the Duchess, "Malays live side by side with all races, peacefully, contentedly and with understanding, under British guidance, but, Your Royal Highness," he ended with a smile, presenting the kris, "You must not draw that weapon right out of its sheath. A drawn kris calls for blood within a year!"

At luncheon the Duchess ate her first Malay tiffin. A succession of exotic, highly-seasoned dishes, ended with Gula Malacca, a traditional sweet composed of cold sago, coconut milk and molasses.

After luncheon the Duchess drove thirteen miles into the jungle, to the barbed wire and machine-gun guarded Durian Tunggal sector of the Bertram Rubber Estate to see the manager, Mr. W. G. Ross and his London wife who lived in day and night risk of their lives from terrorists.

Five policemen had been murdered there a year before. Hundreds of trees had just been slashed by Communists out to ruin the rubber industry. A terrorist with a price on his head had been shot dead only a few weeks before.

In this ruthless atmosphere of murder and tension, Mr. and Mrs. Ross slept each night in a locked, mosquito-proof cage with a Sten-gun and a revolver at their sides. Their bungalow was ringed by a high, barbed-wire fence. The stockade perimeter was lit nightly by the white beams of fourteen searchlights blazing into the jungle. Every hour, between dusk and dawn, a great brass gong boomed out the hammer-strokes of "All's well" as the police went their rounds.

A sharp-shooter could lurk in any tree-top, behind any rock.

No wonder a good many people in Malaya thought that the Duchess should not be allowed to go to Durian Tunggal.

Thus, when the Duchess, cool and smiling, was walking through a grove of sad, grey-trunked rubber trees, laughing with her host, a sharp explosion suddenly rang out!

An instant of icy fear. Men's hearts almost stopped beating. The Duchess did not flicker an eyelid. She went on chatting and smiling. It was the Royal touch.

The "shot" was no more than a flashlight photographer's bulb exploding. But, among the rubber trees, bullets were far commoner than flashlights.

That one trivial incident, when nerves were on edge and security at top tension, emphasized the latent danger, the day-to-day risks.

The story of the Duchess's coolness went by bush telegraph into the far hills.

Next morning, October 7th, she and the Duke drove in bullet-proof cars through forty miles of forest, jungle and foothills, climbing, ever climbing, until they reached the tiny village of Kuala Kubu Bahru, high up in a desolate pass, the one strategic gateway which connects the State of Selangor with the wild and savage country of Pahang. It is the country of the tiger and the clouded leopard, the great Indian bison or gaur which stands more than six feet high, the sambhur deer and poisonous snakes by the hundred. So, apart from the risk of bandits, there was no lack of nature's own hazards.

A far worse one had been discovered early that morning. An advance patrol of troops and police, scouting along either side of the jungle road, found a newly dug ambush of slit trenches high on a hillside. Fifty men could there have commanded the road along which her car was to come. Fifty rifles or machine-guns could have blasted her convoy with a hail of bullets.

Luckily the R.A.F. bombing "strafe", three days before, had ferreted out the Reds and put them on the run. But for that the Duchess would almost certainly have been killed.

Outside the village the First Battalion of her own regiment, The Queen's Own Royal West Kent Regiment, was drawn up for inspection. Rank after rank of tanned, lean young men in black berets and stained shorts and shirts of jungle green. Men who lived with a finger on the trigger.

The Duchess addressed them standing facing a wooded hill not fifty yards away, from whose cover, only a short time before, terrorists had raked the camp with rifle fire. It was searched to the last bush before she arrived. Even so, in that wild country, a stray sniper might have been overlooked. The risk of death could always be just around the corner.

She spoke to the men for a long time, walking down the ranks, pausing here and there to talk to different men about their experiences, their families, their future hopes.

Meanwhile the Duke of Kent was away on the rifle range, having a high old time blazing at targets with every sort of weapon from an Owen gun to a Sten.

"Why have you been so long, Mummy?" he asked when he came back. "I have very little of my own, but *these* are my men," his mother answered simply. That quiet remark said everything.

When, at last, they got back to Singapore the young Duke found the most wonderful birthday party waiting for him. Mr. J. F. Nicoll, the Governor of Singapore, now Sir John Nicoll, staged a party which neither the Duke nor anyone else who was there will ever forget.

There were only twenty guests, including the Duchess and Mr. Malcolm MacDonald, Commissioner-General for South-east Asia, with a good sprinkling of young midshipmen from the Navy in Singapore harbour.

The dinner was all-Chinese. It included a felicitously-named soup, Shui Pi Nan Shan, which means, "May you Live as Long as the Southern Mountain".

Then there was a dish of almond chicken, served with "thousand-year-old eggs". Actually they are no more than a year or two old, and somewhat fresher in taste than many which wear the British Lion. This was followed by shark's-fin omelette, bamboo shoots and fried rice.

Everyone ate with chopsticks from round bowls, the newcomers were allowed to use spoons when the chopsticks became too much for them.

Then the Duke blew out the seventeen candles on his cake and cut it with a parang, a ferocious Malay knife given him two days before by Iban trackers attached to the Royal West Kents.

For the next four days the Duchess had not a minute to call her own. She attended a youth rally, driving through a half-mile avenue packed with no less than 23,000 yelling children. The noise was deafening, the enthusiasm electric.

She was the centre figure at two garden parties. Two thousand two hundred guests turned up at one of them—the biggest party ever held in the history of Singapore. She had a smile or a handshake for every-one presented to her. She made a graceful speech at an official dinner. She inspected a war cemetery and she planted a tree. All very wearing. And all in the humid atmosphere of an overheated greenhouse. "I love the heat," she said.

Meanwhile, the Duke had the time of his young life. He drove a bulldozer. He flew in a Meteor jet fighter. He raced round the park of Government House on a police motor-cycle. He went swimming and sailing. And he took enough photographs to fill a dozen albums.

The Duchess's waking hours were spent standing on platforms, sitting in open motor-cars, walking through cheering, perspiring crowds, receiving endless guests, with, once or twice, an hour in a shop or a late dance in a night-club to round off the day.

On any of those occasions she could have collected a bullet. So, when early on Tuesday, October 14th, she boarded an R.A.F. Sunderland flying-boat, many a heart in Malaya beat more easily, many an official breathed more freely. They had lived on a razor-edge of anxiety.

The result of that tour was that not only the rajahs and tribal chieftains but the everyday people of Malaya, born of a swarm of different races, were cheered, strengthened and inspired by the dignity, charm and beauty of their Royal visitor. She did what no statesman could have done. She brought the Royal touch—above politics, transcending all racial feeling.

Among the local rulers presented to her were the Sultan of Perak, the Sultan of Kedah, the Sultan of Pahang, the Yang di-Pertuan Besar of Negri Sembilan, the Rajah of Perlis, the Sultan of Kelantan, the Sultan of Trengganu, the President of the Regency of Selangor, and the Resident Commissioner of Malacca, Mr. H. G. Hammett. All of them dined with the Duchess for the first time in history.

The good will engendered by that visit endures to this day.

From Singapore the aircraft flew 500 miles across what novelists describe as "the shark-infested China Sea". And shark-infested those South China Seas are. It would go ill with the passengers of any aircraft which came down.

The next stop was Kuching, capital of that prehistoric territory of Sarawâk where the heads of one's enemies are still the prize heirlooms of discerning native families. No member of the Royal family had ever before visited Sarawâk. For three generations it had been ruled feudally and absolutely by its own unique dynasty of "White Rajahs", the Brooke family.

When Sir Charles Vyner Brooke, last of the White Rajahs, formally ceded his "kingdom" to the Crown in 1946, he relinquished his rule over 614,000 natives dwelling in a country fifty thousand square miles in extent. His ancestor, the first White Rajah, had been granted the country by the neighbouring Sultan of Brunei in 1841. In 1864 Great Britain recognized it as an independent State. Twenty-four years later it was placed officially under British protection.

This wild, mountainous country whose peaks rise to 20,000 feet in height is inhabited by the Sea Dyaks (Ibans), and Dyaks, Malays, Chinese, Melanaus, Kayas, Kenyahs, and lesser tribes. Many never see a white man from one year's end to another.

Head-hunting still occasionally flourishes as a popular sport in the wild hills of the interior. The more lucrative products are rubber, oil, sago, rice, gold, pepper, rattans, and birds' nests for soup.

Under the Brooke dynasty, Sarawâk was well governed, happy and full of pride. Then, during the war, it was overrun by the Japanese who slaughtered, tortured, and imprisoned thousands of inhabitants.

Came the end of the war, and, to the distress of many, Sir Charles Brooke decided to abdicate and cede his State to Britain as a colony. The degree of bitterness produced was intense.

Thus, when the Duchess decided to pay a visit, six years later, she was treading on delicate ground. The old resentment at the loss of independence had by no means died down. Britain needed "an Ambassador-Extraordinary" to smooth things down.

As the great Sunderland flying-boat touched down on the muddy Kuching River, it was besieged by scuttling fleets of native praus and sampans, fluttering with flags, paddled by long-haired Sea Dyaks whose faces, leathern, fine-graven by wind and sea-spray, were the faces from another, a prehistoric world. Their chant of welcome, weirdly beautiful, floated shrilly across the river, was flung back by the encircling hills. An other-worldly scene.

The Duchess stepped into the Royal barge and was paddled over the muddy waves to the Astana, the original palace of the Brooke Rajahs. On shore the ground was packed almost as far as eye could see, with tribesmen from the mountains and the inlets of the sea. Some had taken three weeks to travel there by canoe and on foot through dim, green jungle trails, haunt of elephant, leopard, rhinoceros, wild pig, and the great dark-brown bantin, or wild ox.

These primitive tribesmen, with their wives and daughters, dressed in multi-coloured garments, their forearms ringed by bracelets, bright necklaces about their throats, came wearing head-dresses made of the feathers of the hornbill, with leopard-skin cloaks slung over their shoulders.

They brought her, as wild men had brought to Queen Sheba of old, long, thin spears; wave-bladed daggers; poison blow-pipes; native pottery; gold and silver ornaments. One little party of tribesmen, who had been travelling for weeks through dense forests, flowering mountains, paddling down the swirl of shouting mountain torrents, brought her a pathetic gift. A brightly-coloured straw hat.

"It is a thing of no value," they said, casting down their eyes in shame at their poverty.

The Duchess took it with a bow, a charming smile. Then she placed it on her head—and wore it. That one simple gesture brought tears of gratitude to the eyes of the wild little men from the hills.

It was a crowded ten days in Borneo and Sarawâk. The Duchess was able to move more freely than she had done in Malaya. Her eyes missed nothing.

Reviewing a company of soldiers in jungle-green, she pointed to one man's medal and asked him how he won it. The delighted native, Awang Anak Rawang, all smiles and teeth, promptly told her through an interpreter how he had been awarded the medal for outstanding gallantry against the terrorists in that green hell in Malaya.

She went on to Sibu and there saw the rare, traditional parade of young maidens, copper skinned, demure, as their dresses glittered with shining silver coins.

A Dyak headsman who was presented grinned all over his face as he lifted a gruesome lock of human hair which swung at his sword-belt. It had belonged to a Japanese officer whom he had beheaded. Scalps up to date!

Apart from such picturesque native sights and functions, the Duchess put in her usual programme of hard work. One civic ceremony followed another, each meant an introduction and a speech, dozens of handshakes and a quick interest in everything and everyone.

At Jesselton, capital of North Borneo, she drove to open the first teachers' training college, preceded by a wild escort of mounted Baja chieftains, waving their pennoned lances and screaming blood-thirsty war-cries.

There, too, she opened the new police barracks, costing nearly half a million pounds, named Marina Barracks after her. She treasures to this day two century-old Chinese scrolls which were presented to her to mark the occasions.

Then there was a garden party for people of all races and colours at which hundreds of guests, Chinese, Malays, Borneans, and the tribesmen from the hills, mingled with the white population. Again, "racial segregation" was unknown.

Sandakan was once a town. When the Australian troops swarmed in at the end of the war and drove the Japanese out with bomb and bayonet, the town was razed and burnt to the ground. Today it has arisen like the Phoenix from its ashes. There the Duchess opened the new Duchess of Kent Hospital which has meant an enormous step forward in health services to the native population.

The Royal party then went on to Brunei, the Sultanate which, in 1841, gave the original grant of territory and government to the first White Rajah of Sarawâk.

Today, Brunei is infinitely smaller than the territory which it gave away. A total population of under 41,000 inhabits 2,226 square miles, whilst the capital town, Brunei, has a population of less than 11,000. A British Resident advises the Sultan, H.H. Sir Omar Ali Saifuddin, K.C.M.G., on administration.

The Sultan, who was recently in London, is an alert, youngish man with dark hair and a moustache and smart, horn-rimmed spectacles.

He gave the Duchess and the Duke a thoroughly Oriental welcome. She was carried through the streets in a State litter, sitting beside the Sultan, whilst in front, carrying flags and beating brazen cymbals, marched the white-clad Royal Regalia Bearers. The beating of drums, the dull booming of gongs, the shrill cheers of hundreds of school-children, were followed by an address of welcome which the Sultan, in glittering traditional dress, read to the Duchess whilst she sat en-throned on the Royal dais.

Then came a pageant of Eastern splendour which surpassed anything she had seen before on the tour. Turning to the Sultan, she said:

"I am struck by the similarity between our two races, for the British, like you, while constantly adopting new ideas, have nevertheless maintained many of their old traditions."

At the State Banquet which followed, she swallowed her words in more senses than one, for she ate curried beef and chicken, drank warm champagne and said she adored it!

Brunei has an oil town named Seria. There they had just drilled a new oil well. So they asked the Duchess to name it "Marina Well".

Fortunately, enterprising newspapermen accompanying the tour, produced a bottle of champagne hung on a string with which she was invited to christen the well.

Picking up the bottle she said: "This is fun"—and scored a direct hit on a narrow drilling bit.

That lighthearted informality which matched so well her regal manner on more solemn occasions, left a last memory with the crowds who saw her off. She was just about to step aboard the Sunderland flying-boat when the slipstream from the Royal baggage plane, just taking off a little lower down the river, whipped her wide straw hat off her head and blew it away.

The Duke of Kent has always been a keen ski-ing enthusiast. In 1961 the Duchess, Princess Alexandra and Field-Marshal Viscount Montgomery were among those who watched the Duke competing at St. Moritz in the British Army Downhill Ski Championships

The Duke of Kent's wedding to Miss Katharine Worsley: (*above*) a pre-wedding family group; (*left*) the bride and groom leaving York Minster after the wedding

The Duchess's parting peal of laughter crowned a visit which Brunei will never forget.

There followed a week-end at Singapore and then a heavy programme of official engagements in Hong Kong, where enormous schemes of post-war construction were under way. There, on the threshold of Communist China, she carried out six days of virtual "hard labour", laying foundation stones, inspections, opening ceremonies, official dinners and the rest.

She carried it all out with that Royal dignity and personal charm which made every man and woman present feel that they were important.

Not least was the profound impression she made on the resident Chinese population of Hong Kong, who depend for their living on British trade and the stability of British rule.

When the Duchess and her son finally flew off from Singapore on November 9th, they left behind a legacy of good will, affection and loyalty which no politician, trade mission, or ambassador could possibly have created.

Her photograph was pasted into countless albums. It hangs today on thousands of house walls, even in the village "long houses" of the Dyaks, hidden in remote jungles of Borneo where no white man sets foot.

Malays are Mahommedans and most of the Sarawâk tribesmen are pagans. Christmas cards mean nothing to them. Yet bright shopkeepers in Kuching did a roaring trade selling Christmas cards bearing a portrait of the Duchess!

Her dresses and hats, for long the pattern by which discerning London set its styles, were copied by bazaar tailors in every street in Singapore and Hong Kong, every town in Malaya and Borneo.

And today, hundreds of girls born in bamboo huts in the steaming jungles of Malaya and Borneo, are called Mirian, which is the nearest that the Malay tongue can get to Marina.

That, perhaps, was the best compliment of all.

At home, the day-by-day reports of this Royal progress through bandit-infested jungles, in humid heat, under brazen suns, carried out by a woman who, to deaden her sorrow, had dedicated her life to the service of her adopted country, caught the public imagination. It had the ring of old and high adventure—the Elizabethan touch.

She came home to a London that, not for the first time, took her straight to its heart.

The Government gave a State luncheon in her honour at the Mansion House on December 16th, 1952.

That morning, a guard of honour of her own regiment, the Queen's Own Royal West Kents, marched proudly, with bayonets fixed and colours flying, from the Tower of London to the Mansion House. There the Duchess, who had seen their comrades in action on the rim of the world, inspected them.

Mr. Oliver Lyttelton, now Viscount Chandos, who was then Secretary of State for the Colonies, presided at the luncheon. The Duchess was received by the Lord Mayor, Sir Rupert de la Bere.

Among the guests were the Archbishop of Canterbury; the Prime Minister, Mr. Winston Churchill; Lord Swinton; Mr. Attlee; Mr. Clement Davies; the Sultan of Johore; the High Commissioners for Australia, South Africa, Ceylon, Pakistan and Southern Rhodesia.

Mr. Lyttelton, proposing a toast to the Duchess, said what everyone had felt—that the programme had been too great a call upon her strength and health. He, like the rest of us, was delighted to see that she had not only survived it but carried it out with enthusiasm, energy and serenity.

In her reply, the Duchess put her finger on the mainspring of the British Commonwealth when she said:

"Mr. Lyttelton has said something of the affection which peoples of all races throughout the Commonwealth feel towards the Queen, and I would like to confirm that this loyalty and devotion to the Crown, and to the great family of nations which it represents, was what impressed me most profoundly wherever I went—one was very conscious of a great tide of feeling everywhere spontaneously expressed—and that was something which I found deeply moving, and indeed, remarkable, at this time of material change and spiritual unrest."

An American journalist who was at the luncheon, summed up the reactions of thousands when he said, spontaneously:

"Say, that Duchess of yours is sure the hardest unpaid worker in the world."

CHAPTER TWELVE

Today

TODAY PRINCESS MARINA is a dedicated woman. Her life is given to her children and her Royal duties. Her deep sense of religion, of which she makes no parade, is her anchor and strength. She lives on a very modest private income, less than that of any other adult member of the Royal family, far less than that of many a prosperous business man. Her domestic staff is cut to a minimum.

Her apartments in Kensington Palace are largely offices. There she transacts her official business. Her South American tour in 1959 alone meant writing many hundreds of letters and hundreds of telephone calls. I have seen the files—they cover the end of one office. Her normal working day begins at 8 a.m. and frequently does not end before midnight. If she can call two days a week entirely her own she is lucky.

The rest of her rooms in Kensington Palace are, as I have said, used for official entertainment and for her own eating and sleeping in London. Thus little of her time and living space are truly her own.

After the Duke died she faced the hard fact that she had to live on a severely reduced income.

The old, happy plans for a bigger, more gracious house, vanished on the Duke's death. Few people outside her own friends know that they had planned to sell Coppins—it was actually in the market for a short period. They had hoped to buy Dropmore, that classically lovely eighteenth-century mansion in Buckinghamshire, then in the market. Now it belongs to Lord Kemsley.

A house of supreme elegance, it would have been the perfect frame for the exquisite furniture they had collected with such love and discrimination. A dream which vanished at the drop of the auctioneer's hammer when the treasures had to be sold at Christie's.

The Duchess put all that firmly out of her mind.

"There and then she quite definitely dedicated her life to her children and to carrying on the duties and public work which had been nearest and dearest to the Duke's own heart."

That was told me by one of her closest friends.

"The children's education was provided for by trust funds left by their father, but her own income was cut to ribbons."

In the years that have passed she has brought up the two princes and Princess Alexandra in a thoroughly down-to-earth democratic way, but with a proper sense of their own inherited responsibilities.

As small children they went to a small local school at Iver, usually riding there on their fairy-cycles. Prince Edward and Princess Alexandra made special friends with the twin boys of the local doctor. They had other neighbours' children to tea and visited them in their own homes. When they went to the seaside they stayed in small hotels and played on the beach with the other children. On holiday in Scotland the two boys even helped the local butcher at Ballater to make his sausages. No Royal fence of privilege was set round them.

Prince Michael early had a natural flair for geography which so pleased Queen Mary that she sent him a special set of pictorial maps.

Today the Duke of Kent has grown into an uncanny likeness of his father. He has the same charm which made Prince George the darling of the "twenties", the same devil-may-care youthfulness which made his father the favourite brother of the Prince of Wales. The same zest for life and speed—fast cars, ski-ing, dancing, modern music, lively parties, practical jokes. And he has too, his father's decisiveness of manner, the same underlying sense of duty. He is a man and not a playboy.

His car crashes have, naturally enough, given the Duchess nervous shocks and anxiety. But, like every realistic mother, she faces the fact that if young men are worth their salt they walk hand-in-hand with risk. The Duke inherits his fearlessness from his mother as well as his father.

"I don't think she knows the meaning of the word fear," a close friend told me. "Anxiety, yes—fear, no! That is why she has never molly-coddled the children."

Prince Michael has grown into a very serious-minded young man for his age. Brought up without fuss or fads in simple English values, he has a strong sense of discipline and charming manners. Family love and devotion has moulded his character. He is utterly without "side" and, under his seriousness, full of fun—as good a mimic as his mother.

His father's love of music showed in him when he was a tiny child at school in Iver. There he played the tambourine in the school percussion band with a perfect sense of time and rhythm.

King George VI roared with laughter at the end of the first week at school when his little nephew rushed up to him and said, excitedly: "We've got a pincushion band at our school and I'm playing the tangerine in it."

Today he has graduated from the "pincushion band" to the opera and concerts which he often attends with his mother.

His childhood ambition was to join the Fire Service! Many a time he wandered into a strange fire station, asked endless questions and made firm friends with firemen who had not the slightest idea who he was.

"He is a good sailor, loves the sea, and he's done quite a lot of small boat sailing, whilst Princess Alexandra and the Duchess are more like sisters than mother and daughter," I was told by one in daily contact with them. "The relationship is quite extraordinarily deep—the closest ties of affection and understanding."

Princess Alexandra has inherited her mother's grace and youthful beauty. The same calm poise and quick sense of humour. The glorious eyes and rose-fresh colouring. The flair for dress, decoration and art. The poise and natural manner. The inbred courtesy and consideration for other people. The inborn sense of Royal dignity. And the same abiding, but never obtrusive, deep faith in God and divine justice.

"You never hear the Duchess speak with bitterness of the tragedies and bitter blows which have struck at her family and her own life," a friend told me years ago. Her father once said:

"Few people can realize that Royal families are just human beings; their 'blue' blood just as red as anyone else's; their tears every bit as bitter . . . to be born a prince (or princess) is an accident but not always a privilege and by no means a career."

Those words apply to her today—with the difference that she had made her life a dedicated career in the service of Britain and has brought up her children to go in the same way. Her closest friend said to me:

"I have never once seen her lose her temper in the many, many years I have known her. She is the fairest person on earth. She makes allowances for everyone's failings and never condemns a person out of hand.

"Yet she always has about her that great 'thing' of Royalty. You would sense that she is Royal if you met her without knowing who she was. Yet she herself is quite unconscious of this aura—if we can call it that. It's an indefinable air of grace.

"It's just the same with her religious sense—it is a quite natural part of her. She never misses a festival of her church or fails to go to church. At Coppins she attends the village church. In London, St. Mary Abbots, Kensington."

Princess Marina has a specially happy relationship with the rest of the Royal family. She has been "the glass of fashion and the mould of form" for both her nieces for a quarter of a century.

She was the first Royal princess to smoke in public. A small matter today but it meant a lot then. She smoked with poise and dignity. So much poise that eyebrows which began to lift stopped climbing half-way. She calls her cigarette holder "my little pipe". Princess Margaret followed her aunt's example, copied her cigarette holders and uses them still.

More important, she set a new example in Royal dress. The first princess to break away from the old tradition of stiff, formal clothes, she showed that one could be not only regal and dignified but smart at the same time.

At home she is the perfect housekeeper. She runs the house, orders the meals and supervises the costs herself. All her servants have been with her for years. That speaks for itself.

She never forgets or loses her friends but none, except her own family, address her as Marina. Her family, her home, her garden, her music and her friends—these are her relaxation from the hard work of being Royal.

For Royalty, in her case particularly, is an hereditary family business. It means long hours, long training, inherited responsibilities, little privacy.

Always an unending programme of public events which demand unflagging interest in a multiplicity of things and people—from coal-mines to atom-plants; from the launching of a ship to the visitations of incurables, baby clinics, city halls. Factories, farms, New Towns, old Dominions, friendly states and cold-war diplomats. There is no end to it all. The clock ticks remorselessly.

A Lord Mayor retires at the end of his year in office—too often a near nervous-wreck. A Royal Princess never retires. The film star's life is a bed of bouquets by comparison. The statesman is a far freer person. He may be criticized, lampooned, attacked. He can answer back, Royalty never does. It just grins and bears it all.

Above all, Princess Marina has made her mark in the history of this modern age by the sheer impact of her own personality. She has "made friends and influenced people"—millions of them, here and throughout the world.

Had she, as Princess Marina twenty-five years ago, set a fashion for stuffy formality and conscious hauteur it is very probable that Royalty would not be as beloved as it is today.

Her utter femininity; the commonsense upbringing of her children; her smartness without ostentation; her endless official engagements, cheerfully carried out even to the far corners of the world; her dignity and friendliness—all these qualities have built up a living picture in the minds of thousands who have never seen her. The picture of a brave, kindly woman who does a lot of hard work for little material reward.

That is the life and faith of H.R.H. Princess Marina, Duchess of Kent, today.

CHAPTER THIRTEEN

Showing the Flag—South America, Australia, Nigeria, Siam

WHAT IS the purpose of a Royal tour abroad? Why send a hard-working Royal duchess and her delightful daughter, both with an infinity of potential engagements at home? to visit South American States, which were never a part of the British Empire and are certainly never likely to be?

That sort of facile question the unthinking might well have asked when it was announced, early in 1959, that the Duchess of Kent and Princess Alexandra were about to set off on a twenty-thousand-mile visit to Mexico, Peru, Chile and Brazil.

It meant top-speed travel by B.O.A.C. Britannia, constant receptions, State banquets, visits to places of national and civic significance, endless handshakes and invincible good humour. It meant heat and dust, deserts and mountains, peoples of many races. And it all had to be done in six weeks. A tight schedule, as Americans say.

The reason for this arduous pilgrimage was not difficult to determine if one bothered to remember a little recent history.

There was a time, just before the Second World War, when Britain's financial investments and commercial markets in South America were gigantic. In 1939, our investments in Latin-American countries exceeded seven hundred million pounds. Twenty years later when the Duchess paid her visit, those investments had shrunk to a third of their previous value.

That staggering drop was part of the sacrifices Britain made during the war. We sold out our interests wholesale in order to pay for freedom. British railway shares and other enterprises were sold up on a wholesale scale. London ceased to be a fount of capital. Latin-America turned towards the new financial sun in New York.

In addition Britain had to make cuts in her official representation in the various States and cuts in our information services. The result was that many people in Latin-America thought that their countries were no longer of interest to Britain. It was a false impression and did us a lot of harm.

The visit by the Duchess of Kent was therefore part of a new and more positive effort to dispel this feeling held by many Latin-Americans, that Great Britain was losing interest in them. No better Ambassadresses could have been found than the Duchess and her daughter. Their personal charm, ease of manner and innate friendliness were to be of incalculable value to this country's declining prestige in South America.

It was a singularly sad coincidence that the last British Royal visit to Latin-America, should have been that paid by the late Duke of Kent who, as Prince George, accompanied the Duke of Windsor, then Prince of Wales, on a State visit to Argentina in 1931.

It is forgotten by many people that British links with Latin-America go back a long way. In many parts a visiting foreigner is still called "Ingles" or "Señor Mister", no matter what his nationality may be. On the walls of chancelleries and naval clubs in South American cities, there still hang dusty portraits of Canning and Cochrane, reminders of Great Britain's role in earlier Latin-American history.

We forget that British troops, under their own officers, fought with the armies of Simon Bolivar in the wars of independence against Spain. British diplomacy helped to consolidate the new states which were born out of the old Spanish Latin-American empire, and, in 1828, British mediation created Uruguay as an independent state and ended the conflict between Argentina and Brazil.

Thus, the Duchess's visit was a significant link with past history and an important step forward. Today, Britain can afford to pay more attention to those countries. Meanwhile, since the war the United States of America have become Latin-America's greatest trading partner—a dependency which does not please all Latin-Americans.

The vast potential both in trade and friendship offered by Latin-America is best appreciated if one realizes that the sub-continent is two and a half times the size of Europe with a population of 180 million people—an enormous field for long-term enterprises. Yet, today, Britain supplies only about five per cent of Latin-America's total imports. Germany and France have both made far greater strides than this country since the war.

It was a pity that the Royal tour had to miss such old friends as Argentina and Uruguay but, in all the circumstances, the choice of Mexico, Peru, Chile and Brazil, was a good one. All those countries have had their recent troubles and all are emerging from them under new and more progressive Governments.

Mexico, with a population of 33 million people, only emerged from a state of endemic corruption in 1952. The new Government of Señor Lopez Mateos took office, as *The Times* reported, "After one of the most peaceful election campaigns Mexico had ever known." Scarcely a shot was heard or a bomb thrown!

Yet in spite of Mexico's emergence as a well-governed, progressive state, Great Britain's share in Mexico's import trade was only three per cent at the time of the Duchess's visit.

Peru, with a coastline of more than a thousand miles facing the Pacific was, as every schoolboy knows, conquered in the early sixteenth century by Francisco Pizarro, the Spanish adventurer. He subjugated with incredible cruelty the Incas, the now almost legendary ruling caste of the Quichua Indians, who, for five hundred years, had ruled in magnificent state and splendour. They have left fascinating relics of a glittering civilization.

Peru remained under Spanish rule until the country revolted in 1821 and established its independence. The President is elected for six years by direct vote of the people. All adult men and women are compelled to vote.

Although Peru covers approximately 482,000 square miles with a population of more than 10 million people, only about three per cent of the land is cultivated. Agriculture and mining employ seventy per cent of the people. The crops include cotton, potatoes and other vegetables, sugar, fruit, maize, rice, grapes, coffee and corn. It is probable that a far greater area of land was cultivated under the Inca rule. Peru is rich in minerals including lead, zinc, copper, iron ore, petroleum, silver, gold, tungsten, bismuth, antimony and vanadium, of which latter she is the largest producer in the world.

Apart from the ruling fourteen families and the rich upper classes, the standard of living is not high. The average daily wage of a labourer is less than three shillings a day, roughly a pound a week.

The Government, under President Prado, is markedly progressive, and strongly pro-Western.

Since the war, the United States of America had invested over 230 million American dollars in copper deposit in one area of Peru alone—at Toquemala, 10,000 feet up in the Andes. Moreover, Peru has had, in recent years, large loans from the U.S.A. for hydro-electric development and the re-equipment of her ports and railways.

The entire country is physically dominated throughout its length by the soaring majesty of the Andes, peak beyond peak, saddle beyond saddle, mountain after mountain, thrusting its cold beauty more than twenty thousand feet into the clouds.

Chile, the next country on the Duchess's itinerary, is again a state of ancient Spanish origin. No other country in the world can equal the extraordinarily attenuated geography of this snake-like land which extends down the Pacific coast for no less than two thousand eight hundred miles, from the southern tip of Peru to the bleak horror of Cape Horn. The average width of Chile is a mere hundred miles. The entire country is walled off, so to speak, by the great chain of the Andes running along its eastern frontier, rising from five thousand to fifteen thousand feet or more, above sea-level. Robinson Crusoe's island is part of the Juan Fernandez group of islands which lies about three hundred and sixty miles from Valparaiso. The mysterious Easter Island with its hundreds of grotesque stone figures and altars, whose origin is still unknown, is also part of the Chilean possessions.

Chile threw off the Spanish yoke in 1818 and today has a population estimated at round about seven million people. These include four main racial groups; Spanish settlers and their descendants, indigenous Indians, mixed Spanish Indians, and European immigrants.

When the Duchess visited this highly individual and romantic country, it had elected a strongly conservative government for the first time in twenty years, but it was facing a staggering deficit of 225 million American dollars due largely to a sharp fall in the price of copper.

Brazil, the fourth country to be visited by the Duchess, is bigger in total area than the U.S.A.—a giant with growing pains. A Colossus with economic convulsions. Much of the country consists in the north of low-lying forest land and plain but there are many mountain ranges and fertile valleys in the eastern and southern parts. No country in the world can compare in size and length with the Brazilian rivers of which the mighty Amazon alone is 4,000 miles long and has tributaries which are themselves great rivers.

Brazil's wealth consists of a great diversity of large and highly valuable mineral plants. Diamonds and other precious stones are also found. Iron ore deposits are outstandingly rich. Oil has been found and by the time the Duchess's tour had been planned, the annual production was more than two million barrels with prospects of far more to come. Brazil's agriculture, which ranges from coffee, cotton and sugar to bananas, is rich and abundant while she has vast resources of timber, rubber, jute and other things.

This great country of 63 million people is going ahead with the biggest development plans in the whole of South America. They include one of the largest hydro-electric development schemes in the world, roads, railways, industrial expansion in many forms and the building of a new capital city called Brazilia which will open up vast areas of central Brazil.

American, German, French, Italian and Japanese financial and industrial interests have been quick to dip their hands into this rich pie. Brazil, since the war, has relied mainly on American dollars and a constant influx of other foreign capital. Hence the urgent need for Britain to wake up.

The Duchess's visit was, in a sense, the seal upon this country's determination to restore her prestige and develop her trade in Brazil as in other South American countries.

No other country in the world could have sent two more charming members of its Royal family on a mission of such high importance. That fact alone is a salutary reminder of the enormous value of a responsible constitutional monarchy, whose members have a high sense of duty and endearing personality.

Today, our Royal family are, in the most modern sense—Ambassadors-at-Large. They represent this country in the fullest sense, from maintaining friendly personal relations with far distant States, to carrying the flag for commerce. Hence the almost everyday spectacle of Royalty flying at jet-speed to the far corners of the earth. And we take it for granted.

A few years ago when a member of the Royal family went anywhere by air, heads were shaken. Was it worth the risk?

Today the Royal family are all veteran air travellers. B.O.A.C. has greater experience of organizing Royal flights than any other air corporation in the world. At one time in 1960 they were flying no fewer than three groups of Royalty at the same time.

Obviously the organization of such special, high precision flights to various parts of the globe demands meticulous care. B.O.A.C. in the last dozen years has had unrivalled experience.

This is the manner in which a Royal flight to any part of the world is arranged. The first approach to B.O.A.C. on behalf of the Royal family is made by the Minister of Transport and Civil Aviation. He requests that an aircraft be provided on certain dates.

Experts suggest the best aircraft for the particular journey and produce a schedule for agreement by the Queen's advisers at Buckingham Palace.

The scheduling of such a flight is carefully timed. On the day it is adhered to right to the minute.

Once the type of aircraft has been decided, next comes the selection of the crew, interior arrangements of the aircraft, the choice of menus, departure and arrival formalities and many other matters.

Standard layouts are prepared by B.O.A.C. for airliners carrying members of the Royal family. These are amended according to the needs of the flight. The rear cabin will contain comfortable seats to accommodate the official party. Separate from this part are the Royal quarters in the forward part of the aircraft. These usually comprise divans and a dining-room with seats for up to eight people, furnished elegantly but simply.

It is a high honour for a member of B.O.A.C.'s flying staff to be chosen to fly a member of the Royal family. Inevitably photographs of the Captain and others of the crew appear in many parts of the world.

The Captain and his officers are fully briefed on the preparations for the journey. These instructions were more complicated in the case of the Duchess's visit since the Corporation did not then normally operate its aircraft to South America. Today a regular service operates to nearly all South American countries.

The Chief Steward, stewards and stewardesses are also carefully instructed and the menus are agreed with the Royal household beforehand.

In the engineering hangars the aircraft arrives several days beforehand and qualified engineers begin a thorough overhaul, inside and out. On the morning of departure a stubby tractor moves into position and slowly the huge airliner rolls on to the tarmac to the place of honour in front of the Royal Lounge at London Airport.

Fresh flowers decorate the cabins. A pair of wide, shiny steps are rolled up to the passenger doorway. Final touches are added as the Royal limousines glide up to the lounge. Finally, accompanied by members of the Government and others, between lines of photographers, film cameramen and reporters, the Royal passengers follow the red carpet to the foot of the steps. Good-byes are said and a few moments later, after a final wave from the doorway, the engines start up, and right to the minute the airliner taxies away to the end of the runway. All eyes watch as it sweeps along the concrete strip and lifts itself into the sky and is gone.

A signal is received at B.O.A.C.'s headquarters, London Airport, giving the airliner's height, speed, current position and an estimate of when the Commander will reach his next reporting position. All the time the aircraft is airborne these reports flow in regularly. On a map of the world, spread out on a large table, a small model of the aircraft is moved as each position report is received.

Finally, the Captain reports his airliner as in the area of the destination airport. A few moments later his signal says that he has landed and another Royal journey is over. The news flashes round the world and B.O.A.C. records another completely successful Royal operation.

The Duchess of Kent's Bristol Britannia 312 was one of a large fleet of aircraft which fly on B.O.A.C.'s routes from London to the Caribbean and Venezuela, to the United States and Canada, and to East, Central and South Africa.

The interior of the Britannia was specially adapted to accommodate the Duchess and the Princess. Immediately inside the entrance doorway was a semi-circular lounge. The aft cabin was divided into two to provide a dining-room and bedroom. The dining-room was fitted with two tables, each seating four persons. In the bedroom were two divans.

B.O.A.C.'s new colour scheme included a Tiber blue carpet and alternate tweed grey, oatmeal and aquamarine chair covers. Walls were in light grey and the windows had sepia and white chequered curtains.

The commander of the aircraft was forty-nine-year-old Captain Douglas A. Cracknell, a former R.A.F. pilot, and one of B.O.A.C.'s most senior captains. He began flying in 1935 and was a commercial pilot before the war. During the war he served with R.A.F. Bomber Command as Wing Commander of a Pathfinder squadron, gaining the D.S.O. and D.F.C. and bar. He joined British South American Airways (later merged with B.O.A.C.) in 1945 and helped to establish the Corporation's routes to the Caribbean and South America.

The stewardess was twenty-six-year-old Miss Diane Kelly, who before joining B.O.A.C. worked as a secretary in the British Embassy at Mexico City and at United Nations Headquarters in New York.

Other members of the crew were First Officer P. L. Harte-Lovelace, First Officer E. H. Royall, Navigating Officer J. S. Price, Radio Officer E. L. W. Hagger, Engineer Officer R. A. Greisen, Engineer Officer

P. J. E. Ashby, Chief Steward D. Robb, Steward T. Barry and Steward L. Montanes.

The Duchess and Princess Alexandra left London Airport on February 11th, in the Britannia for Mexico. They were accompanied by the Hon. Henry Hankey, Head of the American Department of the Foreign Office, who went with them to translate and advise. Neither the Duchess nor the Princess spoke Spanish but the Duchess, with her quick flair for languages, soon mastered several fluent Spanish phrases which she used with telling effect in some of her speeches. Indeed, the first time she did so, the Mexicans, carried away by enthusiasm, went to the unusual length of interrupting her to applaud the excellence of her accent.

Members of the Household who accompanied her were Lady Rachel Davidson, Lady-in-Waiting, and Mr. Philip Hay, Private Secretary. Group-Captain A. D. Mitchell of the Royal Air Force who has since been reappointed to the Queen's Flight, Sir John Taylor, Director-General of the Hispanic and Luso-Brazilian Councils since 1954 and a former British Ambassador to Mexico, travelled with the Royal Party throughout the tour.

The Duchess's first engagements included lunching with the President of Mexico, receiving members of the British community in Mexico, dining at the British Embassy with the Commonwealth Ambassadors, visiting the University of Mexico City, witnessing a rodeo or charreada, visiting the site of the sacred city of Teotihuacan and generally acquainting herself with the life, customs and commerce of Mexico.

She was then due to fly to Merida in the State of Yucatan on February 19th and drive ninety miles up-country to see the ancient city called Chichen-Itza. There she was due to spend the night.

Next day she had to leave by air for Lima, the rich and stately capital of Peru, dine with the President of Peru, spend five days seeing the sights and activities of Lima and then go on to Cuzco, the ancient capital, after which she was due to spend the night at another Inca city, perched on the edge of a two thousand feet high precipice. Then on to Chile and Brazil. The visit was due to end on March 3rd. It left practically no time for any private, personal enjoyment.

The royal party arrived in Mexico City to be greeted by a milling mob of five hundred newspaper men who stampeded across the airfield in a wave of good humour. The absence of police and soldiery was noticeable.

By an odd coincidence, President Eisenhower had chosen also to pay a visit to the fashionable Mexican seaside resort of Acapulco. He was received with noticeable ceremony.

As the Duchess alighted from the Britannia wearing a dress of brilliant royal blue silk, and a white floral hat, she and Princess Alexandra, in pale blue silk, captivated the crowd instantly. A thunder of cheers was punctuated by shrill cries of *"Bonita"* ("How Pretty").

That spontaneous, warm-hearted welcome more than offset the fact that no guard of honour had been provided and no band played.

The Duchess and Princess drove to the National Palace where they were received by President Lopez Mateos who was accompanied by Señor Manuel Tello, the Mexican Foreign Minister.

Her Royal Highness handed the President a letter from the Queen, in whose name she conferred upon him the insignia of the G.C.M.G. The Foreign Minister was invested with the K.B.E. The President then conferred the Order of the Aztec Eagle on the Duchess and on the Princess.

Later they drove along the Paseo de la Reforme to place a wreath on the Mexican Independence Monument. There, girls from the Maddox Academy, founded by an Englishwoman, Miss Angel, formed a guard of honour, whilst the crowd cheered the Royal party lustily.

Later that day, the Duchess held a reception in the garden of the British Embassy for Mexican and English journalists. Then came luncheon at the Pardo Hotel and a visit to the American-British Cowdray Hospital.

One incident which particularly endeared the Royal visitors to the volatile, warm-hearted Mexican public, was when mother and daughter, clad simply in cotton frocks, sandals and head-scarves, mingled with the peasants and other humble worshippers at the Shrine of Our Lady of Guadalupe.

They were practically unnoticed in the crowd until the whisper went round. Next to them at the shrine was a poor Indian mother who, with her little daughter, shuffled forward to the altar on their knees, confessed their simple sins and asked forgiveness.

The visit to the charreada, an elegant Mexican version of a rodeo, showed them a vivid, daring and highly coloured side of Mexican traditional sport.

Amateur riders dressed in the romantic, traditional style of the cowboys or gauchos of the vast cattle ranches of the country, galloped

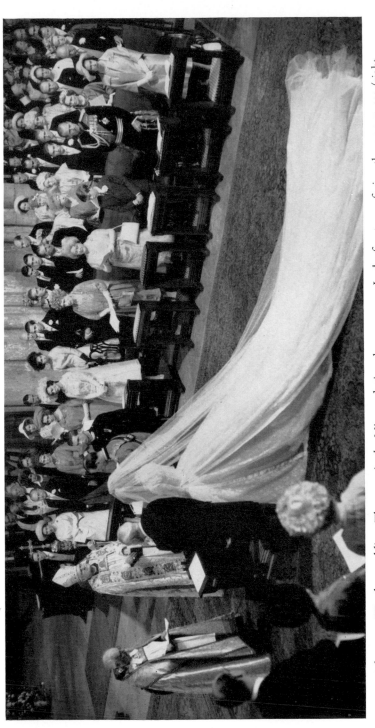

The Kent–Worsley wedding. The scene in the Minster during the ceremony. In the front row facing the camera are (right to left): the Queen, the Duke of Edinburgh, the Prince of Wales, the Queen Mother, the Queen of Spain, Princess Marina, Princess Alexandra, Princess Paul, Prince Paul, Princess Margaret, the Earl of Snowdon. Beside the bride is her father Sir William Worsley and Prince Michael was best man

A recent formal portrait

madly across the arena, chasing bellowing steers, which they caught by the tails and threw instantly.

Another highly diverting and dangerous feat was to jump on wild mares at full gallop without being thrown. After that, the lassoing of wild ponies by the foreleg seemed almost tame. The whole performance was a highly skilled display of daring riding, expert horsemanship and incredible skill of hand and eye with the lasso. The performers were of all ages from six to sixty, and included Mexican girl riders in flowing colourful petticoats riding side-saddle on prancing mustangs.

The Duchess and the Princess were hatless but wore Mexican rebozos or stoles, round their shoulders. These were presented to them by the President's wife and their daughter Eva, and by the wife of the Foreign Minister. Princess Alexandra's stole was of lilac worn over a dark pink dress, a style that is highly popular with all classes of Mexican women.

A bull-fight brass band, obviously delighted with the importance of the occasion and the feminine charm of the Royal visitors, played "God Save the Queen" to the top of its bent, and the Mexican National Anthem, whilst the crowd roared, "*Viva, viva*".

At the end of the performance the entire company of cowboys, women dancers and women riders, rode in pairs before the Royal box. The cowboys, lean, athletic and sun-tanned, wore tight leather jackets and braided brown trousers, sparkling with mother-of-pearl, and elaborately decorated pistol holsters. The girl dancers and side-saddle riders wore vivid costumes which made an unforgettable pageant of colour in bright sunlight.

That night, the Duchess and the Princess attended a brilliant ball which raised £15,000 for the blind. The Duchess was a strikingly regal figure in an old-gold gown sparkling with brilliants. Princess Alexandra looked slim and girlish in a blue floral gown. They danced until nearly three o'clock in the morning.

Then came visits to housing estates, workers' flats, dusty suburbs, humming factories and the Flower Market. There, a small Mexican boy presented the Princess with a rose. Leaping in the air with excitement, eyes and teeth shining, he shouted that never to his dying day would he forget the moment when the lovely English princess had accepted his rose.

There was an amusing moment when Princess Alexandra was visiting the British Industrial Centre. A fair-haired young man, obviously very English, was in charge of part of the exhibition. The

Princess, with the infallible Royal memory for faces, suddenly noticed him, stared hard and said:

"Weren't you . . . ?"

"Yes," the young man answered, "I was."

He was twenty-four-year-old Old Etonian Patrick Tritton. He had been, since leaving Eton and England, a cowboy, lorry driver, horse trader and shop assistant. Princess Alexandra had last seen him at an undergraduates' party at Cambridge some years before. Now the Old Etonian had risen to be Exhibition Manager of the permanent fair run by the British Chamber of Commerce in Mexico City.

Patrick said later: "I'd have loved to have asked the Princess to my flat for a drink. But I simply daren't. You see, I keep a tame ocelot and it's still awfully fierce. It's liable to fly at people and claw them to bits!"

During their visit to the ancient city of Teotihuacan, the Duchess and Princess Alexandra saw the Temple of the Plumed Serpent, decorated in fascinatingly horrific style with stone snakes' heads and gargoyles. The Duchess insisted on climbing to the top of the 220-feet-high pre-Aztec pyramid outside the old city.

When someone suggested that such an exhausting climb at an altitude of 7,500 feet in the fierce heat of the mid-day sun, might be too much for her, she replied, with a chuckle:

"I'm not as old as that yet." And climbed it. At the end of that sun-scorched, exhausting tour, Mexico was, quite obviously, enchanted by the quiet charm and unassuming manner of the two Royal visitors, their dignity and ease.

Lima, a city of a million people far to the south on the Pacific coast of Peru, was the next stop. They flew over the Mexican mountains, over the Pacific, leaving the Panama Canal and the Republics of Colombia and Ecuador to the east and landed in impressive style. Lima, the old and splendid city of the Conquistadores, had never before seen an airliner of such impressive size and power.

A guard of honour was drawn up. A military band blared a brazen welcome.

Señor Raul Porras, Minister for Foreign Affairs; the head of the President's military household; the Mayor of Lima; the British Ambassador; Sir Berkeley Gage and Lady Gage; the Canadian Ambassador and Mrs. Pick; the British Embassy staff and foreign diplomats, were all there to greet them.

The Duchess was a figure of enchantment in a white dress and golden hat. Princess Alexandra wore a blue flowered dress and a blue straw hat. They drove to the Presidential Palace where they were greeted warmly by President Manuel Prado, who presented them both with the Grand Cross of Diamonds of the Order of the Sun, the oldest Peruvian Order. Her Royal Highness gave the President a letter from the Queen and invested him with the insignia of the G.C.M.G. Later she gave the President a token cheque to help relieve the victims of a recent flood disaster.

Then came a State banquet, a meeting with the members of the British community, visits to a hospital, an orphanage, various cultural organizations, a model town for homeless people and an inspection of Markham College, a British Public School run by the British community.

The visit to Cuzco which promised to be of outstanding architectural and antiquarian interest, was, alas, cancelled owing to a sudden railway strike which followed the dismissal of four men who had been accused of responsibility for a railway accident.

However, the Mayor and the Prefect of Cuzco, which is 11,000 feet above sea-level, not to be outdone in courtesy, flew down to Lima specially to present the Duchess with a large carved silver mace of a type used by the Indian authorities. He also gave her a Cuzco painting. Princess Alexandra was given a set of hand embroidered robes similar to those worn centuries ago by princesses of the Inca Court. She tried them on with obvious enthusiasm.

On Sunday, mother and daughter went to church in the morning at the private chapel of the British Embassy. After church, they were driven a few miles down to Anton, a fashionable resort on the coast, where for a blessed hour or two of relaxation, they enjoyed a sail round the bay in a private yacht.

The rest of the official programme included a visit to the ruins of Pachacamac, an important Inca religious centre.

The Royal visit ended with a speech by the Duchess in Lima's City Hall, in which she thanked Peru for its hospitable welcome and expressed the hope that there would be an increase in Peruvian–British trade, and a far greater exchange of visitors and cultural relations. She and Princess Alexandra were presented with silver keys to the city. A charming gesture.

Then the great aircraft took off on the next leg of the flight down the Pacific coast to Santiago, the capital city of Chile. There again, the welcome was warm-hearted, impressive and spontaneous, from a population of nearly a million and a half.

President Jorge Alessandri entertained the Royal party at the Moneda Palace. The Duchess conferred upon him the insignia of the G.C.M.G. and gave him a letter from the Queen.

There was a tour of the city, a ball at the British Embassy at which Her Royal Highness danced with the President and with Cabinet Ministers and got to bed in the small hours.

Later, she visited the great Chilean paper, newsprint and cellulose factory at Puenta Alto, saw a typical worker's home and was presented with a silver salver from the factory workers.

At the height of this exhausting programme, the Duchess and the Princess took a few precious hours off to go by jeep 7,500 feet up into the top of the Cerro Colorado peak. They were 9,000 feet above sea-level.

The next visit was to Valparaiso, a city of nearly a quarter of a million inhabitants, to which they went by air.

There the Duchess reviewed Naval cadets and met an old friend, Señora Violet Price de Munoz, a Chilean-born widow of British descent. She had played on the beach at Bognor Regis as a school-girl with the Duchess and her sisters in those childhood days of exile from Greece.

From Chile, the Britannia flew over the bleak majesty of the Andes across the plains, forests, swamps and rivers of the Argentine and southern Brazil to Rio de Janeiro.

There they were received by President Kubitschek whom the Duchess invested with the Collar and Cross of the Order of St. Michael and St. George.

There followed the usual run of State banquet, entertainments and visits. As before, the Royal visitors were unflagging in energy and undiminished in charm and friendliness.

They flew home on March 15th. B.O.A.C. provided a magnificent service which in itself was a first-class advertisement for British design, engines and air-service.

At the end of it all the Duchess and the Princess landed at London Airport having accomplished a tour of immense national importance and achieved a triumph of personal friendliness. As a newspaper writer remarked: "The tireless Kents have done their part of the job. Now it's up to the City and to British businessmen to follow up the advantages they have created. The keys are in the doors."

The South American visit was, in a sense, Princess Alexandra's baptismal introduction to those long-distance personal visits to foreign countries which are part of the arduous service that Royalty gives to the State.

It was not long before she flew to the other side of the world on her own first great State visit without her mother's support. Not many young women under twenty-three years of age would choose to face a round-the-world trip of public appearance and speeches knowing that they would be the target for millions of eyes, their every word noted and recorded.

That is what Princess Alexandra did in August, 1959, when a few months after her return from South America, she flew to Australia to represent the Queen at the Centenary Celebrations of Queensland. It was no small test of character and poise. All eyes in Australia were on the slim girl with the friendly smile, quick understanding and gentle dignity. One false step or loss of nerve could have created a tide of gossip. Instead Australia was captivated, charmed and, unashamedly, enraptured.

The visit started with the usual planning anxieties and ended splendidly. There is an indefinable border-line where the workings of protocol and programme cease and the human personality of the personage concerned dominates not only the scene but the instinct of the crowd beyond the red carpet. That is the ultimate testing point. The everyday man and woman are the people who decide in their own hearts whether the visitor—Royalty, statesman, politician or anyone else—is a success. In Australia the word is "dinkum" which means, literally, "true".

There were initial criticisms of some aspects of the programme and demands for more and yet more of the Princess's exiguous spare time. Australian newspapers and up-country mayors can be extremely outspoken on such matters.

The Princess flew out in August, 1959, in a B.O.A.C. Comet IV which took her as far as Vancouver, with the prospect of a 35,000-mile tour in front of her. Those in attendance were Lady Moyra Hamilton, her Lady-in-Waiting; Mr. Philip Hay, the Private Secretary; Group-Captain T. N. Stack of the Queen's Flight who was attached for flying duties and Wing-Commander H. B. Kelly as medical officer. They flew by way of Vancouver and then across the Pacific, touching down at Honolulu and Fiji and thence to Australia.

The six weeks' tour included visits to Melbourne, Canberra, Brisbane, Sydney and other great Australian cities, with visits to the lonely out-back country of sheep farms, mines and near-desert.

The tour did not start too auspiciously. Mr. Stevenson Pugh, a well-known journalist who accompanied the Royal party, summed it all up neatly when he wrote:

"When the Princess arrived the newspapers were unanimously growling about the arrangements for her tour. At every hint of too many formal occasions they campaigned vociferously. Sample head-lines: "Anything Goes for Princess Mambo . . . She's In For a Long Handshake . . . Ordeal For Princess . . . Tour needs Night Life . . . Mayors Protest Princess Being Kept In At Night'."

Even the restrained *Sydney Morning Herald* commented: "There has been an amount of controversy unusual even for a Royal tour. It is possible to regret that arrangements have followed the formal pattern of earlier Royal tours quite so closely."

Official Government reaction was to proclaim that the accent of the tour would be on youth. Emphasis was given to the number of young people invited to each function. But it wasn't good enough.

Then Princess Alexandra herself saved the day. She gave an informal introductory Press conference to Australian newsmen in London at which she told them that since the tour was mainly connected with the Queensland Centenary celebrations, it had naturally a serious sig-nificance.

Mr. Pugh commented: "The hint was widely taken here. The mayors of four Queensland towns were allowed to plan Royal balls raising the number in the three weeks' tour to five. There was the inevitable row about who would dance with the Princess, but com-bined with more informal functions it seemed that these plans would work—until the Princess flew into Canberra. An Australian counted the official handshakes at the airport and made it fifty-three."

The Princess gave a reception within twenty-four hours which was attended by the Press after which she attended a ball given by the Prime Minister and Government in Canberra. And she took a day or two's badly needed rest. After that, as Mr. Pugh said:

"Then she emerged and all changed. Continually, Australians have been warmed by her bright, spontaneous personality on their TV screens and the front pages of the newspapers. While they still think she is being cut off from them by official barriers, they have definitely got the idea that she is on their side.

"And with good reason. I have inquired, for example, about the famous occasion when Princess Alexandra sat on the top-hat of Sir Henry Abel Smith, Governor of Queensland. The Princess sat on the hat in the back seat of her car because, following what is now her routine, she strolled away from the red carpet on the cathedral steps to talk to some choir girls who caught her eyes, then walked out into the road on the wrong side of the car to wave both hands at crowds, and then got in by the wrong door.

"The incident would have been unnoticed except that Princess Alexandra delightedly held out the crushed hat and waved it to the crowds.

"She has endeared herself to the tour party and the Press contingent by her friendly informality. She calls them Alexandra's Ragtime Band."

Now for the outspoken verdict of an Englishwoman business executive who lives nine months of the year in Australia, and knows and loves the country. This is how she summed it up to me: "The dinkum Australian has his heart and his natural ties of loyalty in this country. He is incredibly virile, terribly down-to-earth. He loathes pomposity. His country and his business is expanding while you watch. That is why American dollars and high-powered business American teams of trade research experts, statisticians, mining engineers and others are moving in. They have the dollars to invest. The money to plant—the orders to give and the know-how, right on the spot.

"The British too often send out a charming person who has no team of experts with him and can only promise to deliver the goods through his office or from his works, months ahead. Delivery is often overdue. Faults in workmanship or quality are too common. The Federation of British Industries know all about this.

"Princess Alexandra's visit was the best thing that British prestige and trade could have had. The Australians loved her young exuberance, her quick wit and that trace of schoolgirl impishness. Had she been stuffy and formal, the tour could have been a flop. As it was, it ended as a tremendous personal success. They're still talking about her. They simply love the girl."

It was all very well put by the reporter who wrote: "The wonderful performance of our up-and-coming Princess has done so much to put a young and zestful face on the Old Country in the past five weeks."

Perhaps the little incidents of the tour are the things that people remember longest.

Once she stopped her car at dusk on a desolate country road, to talk to one little girl waiting all alone to see her go by.

As a woman journalist wrote at the time in the *Daily Herald*:

"She had a formal job to do: shaking hands, making speeches, touring towns and villages, eating long dinners, dressing up in full regalia for evening receptions and balls.

"She did these things efficiently and charmingly, with a smile—in her eyes as well as on her lips—which suggested she really enjoyed it.

"But it was when things went wrong that she really showed herself in a class on her own.

"When a car moved forward unexpectedly and the door almost knocked her off her feet, when a streamer flung from the Melbourne crowd hit her on the cheek, when crowds mobbed her and cut her off from her escorts, she took it all with composure and smiling, natural dignity.

"Even when she had to speak those long, wordy platitudes which speech-writers insist on putting into the mouths of Royalty, her sincerity came through.

"She wanted to meet ordinary people and she did—in spite of an official programme that was criticized beforehand as far too strenuous.

"All through the tour, she was friendly and helpful to the Press party that followed her.

"And when she left Melbourne—she wasn't ashamed of showing that the vast crowds shouting, 'Come back, soon, Alex', had reduced her to tears.

"Princess Alexandra had a goodwill job to do. She did it brilliantly."

She left Melbourne, cheered along every road from Government House, by thousands of people. Thousands more lined both sides of the road to the airport ten miles away. All through the city, there were almost continuous roars of cheers. When the procession made a short halt at the Town Hall, a snow-storm of torn paper and confetti dropped on the Royal party from office blocks amid cries of, "Come back, Alex."

The Lord Mayor of Melbourne presented to the Princess a volume of colour photographs of the finest scenes in and around the city. Another large cheering crowd had assembled to bid farewell at the airport.

At Canberra airport the Princess was met once again by Sir William and Lady Slim and Mr. Menzies, Prime Minister, and Dame Pattie Menzies. Before the Royal progress to Government House the Princess

opened a new building named after her for the Women's Royal
Australian Naval Service.

Today, Australians remember that when the Princess was at Mount
Isa in Queensland, the centre of a huge mining area, she not only
broke away from the official party to talk to some children who were
waving flags and cheering but, she told a group of bearded miners,
"I will be back here some day." That is what they look forward to. In
Melbourne she said, "I must come back, I have loved it all," and she
meant it.

On the way back to England she stayed for a few days in Siam
where she was entertained by the King and Queen of Siam. Whilst
there she visited the famous Temple of Love at Angkor in Cambodia,
twenty-three miles from a main road, in the heart of the jungle. She
was a little puzzled by the fact that thousands of troops and police
lined the route. Army minesweepers swept the road in front of her.
Crack shots covered every yard of the road. An entire army division
was on duty. No one explained why.

The following day it was revealed that armed bandits had held up
and robbed a British woman diplomat at the temple, just before the
Princess began her tour. Police shot one bandit dead and arrested two
others. It was known that others were at large in the jungle, heavily
armed.

From Siam the Princess flew to New Delhi where she was the guest
of President Prasad of India. There she visited the Red Fort in Old
Delhi—without an escort.

Then came the last leg of the flight home with the knowledge of a
splendid job well done.

Just over a year later, in October, 1960, she flew in a B.O.A.C.
aircraft to Nigeria to put the Royal seal on the birth of independent
Nigeria. After ninety-nine years of British rule, the Union Jack was
struck in Lagos and the green and white flag of the new Nigeria was
run up.

"It was an occasion which only the British could have conceived
and carried out with such poignant dignity," a young Nigerian prince
told me afterwards.

Lagos was decorated on a scale of primitive splendour and sophisti-
cated showmanship. When the Princess drove through the beflagged
streets, lined with cheering Africans and thousands of black children,
it rained in sheets although it was freely rumoured that the local rain-
makers had been heavily bribed to keep the rain away. Officials

wanted the Princess to drive in a closed car from which she could have waved in dry comfort, to the waiting crowds. She insisted upon an open car—and got soaked to the skin.

"That gesture spoke louder than a million words," said the Nigerian *Daily Times*. "She seemed to be saying, 'If the schoolchildren can stand in this rain getting soaked, so can I.' "

At the State Banquet, surrounded by Nigerian ministers and tribal chieftains, the Princess, vividly lovely in a gown of lotus pink, said: "I am going to say what I feel. It is something of an experience to see Africa for the first time in one's life and I do not imagine that the opportunity is given to many people of my age, to visit so important, so respected and so typical a part of Africa as this. During the few days I have spent with you, I have enjoyed myself." That was from the heart.

One of the highlights of that visit was the vividly spectacular performance staged by the Sultan of Sokoto, whose Province borders Dahomey and French West Africa. He organized a Royal durbar for the Princess, who, wearing a diamond tiara and a pale blue silk, full-length gown, watched the spectacle from the Royal stand. Thousands came long distances to watch the procession of horsemen and entertainers pass the Royal stand like fabulously coloured illustrations from fairy tales of long ago.

All the traditional pageantry previously presented to the Queen and the Duke of Edinburgh and Duke and Duchess of Gloucester during their visits to Kaduna, the capital of the Northern Region, was arranged in Sokoto for Princess Alexandra—clowning horsemen, whose docile mounts lay as dead while the riders danced on their recumbent bodies; camels schooled to walk on their knees; acrobatic dancers and groups of men waving writhing, glistening snakes. The leader of these men as he passed the Royal stand tried to horrify the Princess by placing the head of an enormous, wriggling snake in his mouth.

When a group of over-enthusiastic, youthful dancers, in their efforts, surrounded the Royal stand and showed no signs of moving on, the Sultan left his seat, close to the Princess, and sent them on their way.

The durbar ended with the traditional jahi charge across the course. It reached real drama when one horseman was thrown under his horse almost at the feet of the Princess. Although hurt, he insisted that his condition was not serious.

She flew back from Nigeria leaving the memory, as my Nigerian prince put it, "of a very Royal, a very charming and a very human lady. Only Britain could have produced her."

CHAPTER FOURTEEN

The Kent-Worsley Wedding

ON MARCH 8TH, 1961, was announced the engagement of H.R.H. The Duke of Kent to Miss Katharine Worsley, a daughter of Sir William Worsley, Bart., a cricketing squire, of Hovingham Hall in the East Riding of Yorkshire. It was the culmination of the usual crop of rumours which pursue any eligible Royal personage.

One or two other names of charming young women had been suggested by assiduous newspaper gossip writers—those friends to few with but few friends to call their own. But for months, the name of the Yorkshire girl who lived a windswept country life and came relatively seldom to London had been, on and off, steadily in the news.

The man-in-the-street and, more particularly, the average woman, not usually enraptured by Mayfair socialites, international beauties or over-publicized heiresses was, quietly, very pleased about it all. She had a frank, friendly smile and looked as though she knew her own mind. Moreover, her father was a cricketer with his own village eleven and a foot in the M.C.C. What could be better? The English mind is inclined to run like that.

In short, the country was delighted. As the wedding-day drew near it was easy to sense that here was a Royal wedding very near to the people's hearts. It had everything in its favour—and the memory of that other, unforgettable Kent wedding, twenty-seven years before, to bring the bitter-sweet of nostalgia to the middle-aged. We are a romantic people—and a Royal love-story still means much.

The wedding took place three months later on Thursday, June 8th, 1961. True to tradition, our island weather had the last word.

Rain almost spoilt the wedding. It was a typical English day of showers and sunlight. An hour before the first guests arrived at the Minster, the sun came out. Wet grass gleamed. The great bulk of York Minster glowed gauntly in the pale champagne of sunlight. Heroic sightseers who had spent a damp night in sleeping bags, stretched out on the grass round the Minster, began to dry out. They yawned and rubbed their cramped limbs.

Rare occasions, such as this, have always their own distinctive flavour. The essence of this Royal wedding scene was easy to define. It was mainly a family affair, magnificently dressed, splendid to see but, basically, unpretentious.

The mood of the occasion suited the surroundings, for York Minster is not just the Westminster Abbey of the North. In size and in its gaunt perpendiculars, it seems to dwarf mankind. The notes of the organ can fill and dominate the great vault of that soaring interior but the most resonant voices are diminished. There is none of that clutter of statues and stone memorials which makes Westminster Abbey seem smaller than it is, and thus a more approachable place.

One can almost describe the Minster as the new Duchess's parish church. Thus the careful balance which was created between high ceremonial and the minimum of formality was eminently sensible. The order of the processions, for example, was worked out on the principle of "a mixture of precedent and family considerations".

The simplicity of the wedding ceremony was enhanced by the relative scarcity of uniform. True, the Queen's Body Guard of the Honourable Corps of Gentlemen-at-Arms were splendidly impressive with their red tunics and plumed helmets of gleaming gold. But there were a hundred grey top-hats and many a suit of morning clothes had obviously seen long service. Here were the country gentlemen turning up to see the daughter of an old friend being married.

This was not only a Royal wedding but a Yorkshire wedding. The men and women who lined the streets to cheer in the shifting sunlight, were the people of Leeds and Bradford, of York and Halifax with the farmers and farm workers from the broad acres of the Ridings. Had the wedding been at Westminster Abbey, at least a tenth of the on-lookers would have been American. This, however, was no metropolitan occasion but a local one with more than a touch of grandeur.

The voices one heard had the short vowel sounds of the North and not the accents of Ohio. The top-hatted guests were given that canny, knowing scrutiny, as they arrived, which is typical of a Yorkshire crowd. They were weighing up the situation and reserving their enthusiasm.

According to protocol, the junior Royalty arrived first. There was Earl Mountbatten of Burma, with his two daughters, and the Countess of Harewood in a dress of royal blue.

Then came the Crown Princes of Norway and of the Hellenes, Princess Irene of the Netherlands and the Royalty of dynasties overthrown by war and revolution. Among them was Prince Tomislav of Yugoslavia.

Princess Margaret was in the second procession in a loose-fitting coat of ice-blue with a wide Breton hat, swathed with tulle. Her husband wore morning dress.

The Princess Royal wore a lace dress of deeper blue, whilst the Duchess of Gloucester was in red with a gold hat. The Duke of Gloucester and his son, Prince William of Gloucester, were in morning dress.

Then a charming little cluster of bridesmaids and pages, dressed in yellow and white, appeared at the West door, a little awed by it all.

The Queen Mother, smiling in her own irresistible way, walked up the aisle dressed in pale turquoise lace and organdie, her famous pearls and diamonds gleaming. She was accompanied by Queen Victoria Eugenie of Spain, regal in flowered silk.

Then came the bridegroom, tall and slim in the red tunic and full ceremonial dress of the Royal Scots Greys with the blue riband of the G.C.V.O. across his chest. His brother and best man, Prince Michael of Kent, wore the ceremonial uniform of an officer cadet of Sandhurst. Their mother, the Duchess of Kent, was, as always, a most elegant figure, whilst Princess Alexandra looked enchanting in azalea-pink organdie.

Then a fanfare of trumpets heralded the arrival of the Queen. She looked gracious and delightful in ribbed, lilac satin dress, coat and hat. The Duke of Edinburgh was an impressive figure in the scarlet and black uniform of a Field Marshal.

The young Prince of Wales was a model of schoolboy composure in a dark grey suit with a large white flower in his buttonhole. He clasped his hands behind his back precisely as his father does.

The Queen's procession moved at a dignified pace towards the Sacrarium whilst the congregation sang the National Anthem. The Archbishop of York, Dr. Arthur Michael Ramsey, an imposing figure of medieval splendour in cloth of gold cope and mitre, conducted them to their crimson-covered seats near the altar. Opposite sat Lady Worsley, the bride's mother, in pale almond green, with other members of the bride's family.

When the Royal family were finally seated in the front row from left to right were the Queen, The Duke of Edinburgh, The Prince of Wales, The Queen Mother, Queen Victoria Eugenie of Spain, The Duchess of Kent, Princess Alexandra, Prince and Princess Paul of

Yugoslavia, Princess Margaret and Mr. Antony Armstrong-Jones. Behind them were the Duke and Duchess of Gloucester, Prince William of Gloucester, The Princess Royal, the Earl and Countess of Harewood, Earl Mountbatten, the Hon. Gerald Lascelles and his wife, and many foreign Royal guests. These included Prince and Princess Frederick of Prussia, Prince and Princess Georg of Denmark, Prince and Princess Alexander of Yugoslavia and the Crown Prince of Norway.

Meanwhile inside the Cathedral Church of St. Peter, which is the proper name of the Minster, the television cameras had begun to play their part in a programme quite as difficult to administer as the marshalling of the wedding itself. No less than forty-six cameras were employed in the Minster and the city. Some guests were unable to see the marriage ceremony because camera stands blocked the view, but they watched it on monitor screens, which missed no detail. In fine, the television arrangements were masterly. None the less colour television would have done fuller justice to the scene—the glowing crimson and gold of clerical robes, the banked roses in waves of cream and pale yellow, with the White Roses of York and the splendour of red tunics and burnished brass.

Two small incidents relieved the planned ceremonial. The bride, true to the unwritten tradition of all weddings, was a few, a very few, minutes late. Later, there was a subdued rustle of activity among newspaper-men, when it was noticed that the new Duchess had chosen to "obey" her husband. For days beforehand, it had been stated in many newspapers that the order of service to be used would omit the word. "Obey" was not actually included in the published text of the service.

Hence, the puzzled glances which flickered among the 2,000 guests and undoubtedly among many television viewers when the bride promised to "obey" her Royal husband.

Previously, it had been reported that the wedding ceremony would be conducted according to the 1928 Prayer Book version in which the word "obey" is omitted. It is contained only in the 1662 Prayer Book version.

The Dean of York, Dr. Eric Milner-White, later explained why the Archbishop of York had introduced the word into the responses.

It had always been intended that it should be used, he said, because the bridal couple had asked for it. "But it did not appear in the service programme because it is impossible to print bits from the two versions together.

"You cannot amalgamate the two. All we did was to add one or two words at the appropriate point."

A good many guests in the Minster may not have known that any alteration had taken place for the microphones did not carry the responses clearly to all parts of the building.

The setting for the occasion was magnificent. The yellow, cream and white roses splashed colour against the grey stone walls.

The choir in red and white robes, the Gentlemen-at-Arms in scarlet, and gaily-dressed women guests made a river of colour throughout the Minster. Even the television cameras and blazing arc lights could not detract entirely from the scene.

Miss Worsley looked nervous and tense when she arrived. She had run the gauntlet of cheering crowds but the reassuring arm of her father seemed to comfort her.

As the trumpets of the Royal Scots Greys blared in a triumphal fanfare of greeting she began the long walk down the great nave to meet her future husband. She gained confidence with each step.

The bridegroom, tall and resplendent in the dress uniform of the Scots Greys, was a model of self-possession. He chatted cheerfully with his brother Prince Michael, who looked distinctly contemplative.

Every now and then, the Duke glanced eagerly at the door through which his bride would appear. A chuckle ran through the congregation at his expression of delight when she arrived.

During the ceremony, the Duke, clearly alive to the bride's nervousness, encouraged her with smiles and friendly sideward glances.

The two figures seemed almost lost in the great Minster, but their responses to the Archbishop of York were spoken clearly and firmly.

The chief bridesmaid, Princess Anne, was a model of self-possession and dignity, occasionally glancing at her brother, the Prince of Wales, seated with his mother and Prince Philip.

The bridesmaids followed her lead, although the pages, like all small boys at weddings, appeared a little disinterested in the proceedings.

The bride was the climax of this tapestry of splendour, fashion and dignity. The white cloud of her veil and the shimmering magnificence of her fifteen-foot train transformed the scene into one of pure romance.

Her wedding dress was a triumph of splendid simplicity.

The fabric was a silk gauze woven with iridescent thread made specially for her in France.

It gleamed with the brilliance of mother-of-pearl or fish scales. No less than 273 yards of silk, including chiffon mounting, went into this dress.

Her diadem, tilted forward, reminded many people of Princess Marina's own wedding headdress.

The veiling echoed exactly the bride's engagement day hairstyle, which swept straight back from her forehead. The veil was finely pleated under the diadem and floated around her face and shoulders.

There was an instant later on when the long veil and the long train gave the bride an anxious moment. The fabric caught on something as she walked down the aisle after the ceremony. For one dreadful second, it looked as though veil and diadem would crash to the floor.

The new Duchess stopped, twinkled at her husband as the fabric was freed, and then continued her stately walk to the Minster door.

The bridesmaids were straight from the pages of Kate Greenaway. Demurely Victorian, they wore white organdie dresses with tucked bodices, caped and ankle-length skirts. Yellow rosebuds were embroidered on the dresses and set in the small girls' hair.

The pages, in white satin knickerbockers, also wore yellow sashes with yellow rosettes at their knees.

Yellow roses were the only note of colour among the country-looking sprays of white rambler roses.

This wedding seemed to emphasize the fact that the Royal family leads fashion of the better sort, for nearly three-quarters of the guests in the Minster echoed the Royal choice and wore plain-coloured dresses and matching coats.

Many hats were clusters of flower petals, small and head-hugging, and a blessing to those sitting behind. The Queen Mother, the Duchess of Gloucester and Mrs. Gerald Lascelles chose this style. The few cartwheel hats were side-swept and the few Bretons were of shiny straw.

Many of the dresses were in organdie or tulle, in soft cloud shapes which gave grace to the glowing Minster. The wife of the Lord Mayor of London, Lady Waley-Cohen, wore coral in this style.

Every wedding has its moment of parental pathos. This one was no exception. The Duchess of Kent, mother of the bridegroom, wept, as countless mothers have done at other weddings. When she and Princess Alexandra arrived, they both knelt a minute in prayer as they took their seats. They were the only Royal guests to do so.

The Queen Mother, as if she knew the strain the Duchess must feel, leaned across Queen Victoria Eugenie and said a few welcoming words. Prince Philip, too, went out of his way to greet her warmly.

She looked fairly composed at first, but as the minutes ticked by and the bride's car was due she glanced anxiously at the West Door as if nervous that the bride might be late and keep the Queen waiting.

She turned her head to see where her sons were—but they were out of sight behind a stone pillar.

Princess Alexandra turned to her mother several times as though urging her to relax.

But though surrounded by a Royal family who love her dearly, Princess Marina, as she is now known, was on that day a woman alone with her memories.

When she saw her elder son stand by the altar, the living image of the man she had married in Westminster Abbey nearly twenty-seven years ago, it was all too much for her.

Tears came when her son placed the plain gold ring on his bride's finger and she herself became once again Princess Marina.

They were very discreet and dignified tears.

She stood only three steps from her son. Her eyes never left his face. Once or twice they closed in silent prayer. As the Duke made his vows, "With this ring I thee wed," the Duchess was overcome with emotion. She reached for her little coffee-coloured handbag, opened it, took out a tiny white handkerchief and dabbed her eyes.

A brief, homely, dignified gesture, unnoticed by most of the guests.

By the time the register was signed and the Royal party returned to public view, Princess Marina was fully composed. She smiled at some of the guests as she walked down the aisle on Sir William Worsley's arm. But it looked as though each smile was an effort.

Apart from that moment of understandable distress, Princess Marina looked, as usual, regal and dazzling. A large cartwheel hat of osprey feathers seemed to float on her chestnut hair.

Her gown was of caramel organdie embroidered with gold silk thread and diamonds and topazes. It sparkled as she walked. Pearls and crystals gleamed at her neck. Her diamond ear-rings and diamond wrist-watch caught the shafts of sunlight.

She was easily the best-dressed woman in the Minster, filled though it was with fashionable women.

Thus, this Yorkshire wedding which meant so much to the English-speaking world, went as weddings will. Whilst the register was being signed, small boys, growing a little bored, fidgeted. Instantly they were pinpointed on millions of television screens. Prince Charles, much taller than when he attended Princess Margaret's marriage a year before, comported himself with great dignity.

Then came Gustav Holst's "Alleluia" sung with rare effect. Throughout the ceremony, the twelve impressive figures of the Queen's Body Guard of the Honourable Corps of Gentlemen-at-Arms stood impassive, like splendid statues from the coloured past. The plumes of their helmets moved slightly in occasional gusts of air. Otherwise they might have been carved in stone.

Then it was time to go. The procession moved in slow dignity towards the West door. The bride's face, now unveiled, showed by the quick smile that she had lost all her nervousness. The Duke was clearly very happy.

Thus the tapestry, so to speak, unwound again, from the bride's parents, past the Queen—to whom the bride made the most stately curtsey—past the Princess Royal and the Duke of Gloucester, past Princess Margaret and her husband. Then the erect figures and watching faces of the princes and princesses of regnant and dethroned European monarchies. The stately progression was made to the dulcet, if a little restrained, figurations of the toccata of Widor's fifth symphony.

When the couple appeared at the West door of the Minster, there came a roar of cheers and applause from those who waited outside. A guard of honour of the Royal Scots Greys formed an archway of swords. The Duke and his new Duchess walked slowly beneath that arch of steel blades. They looked at each other and smiled. As she entered the car the new Duchess had some little difficulty with that superb and shimmering train, but an attendant helped her to get it into the car.

Thus in the space of one hour and twenty-four minutes, the first Royal wedding in York Minster for 633 years was performed, seen and marvelled at. Outside, a taxi-driver remarked: "Back to normal now."

They drove off to the tunes of "Wooed, Married and All" and "I Have a Wife of My Own". The Queen had lent them her new Rolls-Royce with a transparent roof. So the crowds lining the twenty miles of roads to Hovingham, saw the squire's daughter drive home, regal, smiling, radiant with happiness, very much a Royal lady.

Two thousand guests attended the reception which was held in a marquee at the Hall, a hundred yards long. There were no speeches, no display of presents. It was all quite informal.

There was champagne and caviare, smoked salmon and chicken, strawberries and cream. A five-tier wedding cake was decorated with the initials "E" "K" and the rampant lion of Kent. Mr. Marcus Worsley, the Duchess's eldest brother, called for a toast to the bride and bridegroom. Then a ceremonial sword was handed to the Duke and everyone cried "Push" as he and his wife made the first cut.

Later when the champagne had been drunk and laughter and talk was at full tide, they walked across the sunlit lawn to the Hall to change.

The new Duchess wore a going-away coat of blue over a blue and green floral silk dress and a green hat. The Duke was in a grey flannel suit with the White Rose of York in his buttonhole. The Queen gave them an affectionate good-bye in the Hall, and as they drove off, the Duke of Edinburgh, Prince Charles, Princess Anne, Princess Margaret and a host of others waved them off in the bright sunlight, whilst two pipers played the regimental march of the Royal Scots Greys.

The bells of the village church rang out in a peal that set the jackdaws on wing. The villagers cheered. And the gleaming, half-transparent Rolls-Royce slid smoothly off for the R.A.F. station at Linton. There a Heron of the Queen's Flight took off and flew them to Dyce Airport, Aberdeenshire. Thence they were to go to Birkhall on the Royal estate at Balmoral for the first part of the honeymoon.

After the aeroplane took off, the Royal couple drank to each other in champagne 8,000 feet above the hills and moorlands of the North. For in their fluorescent-red Heron of the Queen's Flight they found three bottles of 1955 champagne and a pile of smoked salmon sandwiches—provided at the Queen's special request.

The only other passengers were their pet dogs—the Duchess's poodle, Charles, and the Duke's Golden Labrador, Columbus.

Aboard the plane were evening newspapers with reports and pictures of the wedding. Piloted by Squadron Leader "Jacko" Jackson, thirty-eight, the Heron flew the 268 miles in ninety minutes, passing through a thunderstorm over Scotland.

At Dyce Airport, hundreds of people greeted the couple with a storm of cheering. The Duke and the Duchess—radiant and without a vestige of strain—smiled and waved. Then they entered their car and drove fifty miles to Birkhall, on the Balmoral estate, where they spent their first ten days.

All Aberdeenshire seemed to line the roadside. Flowers and confetti were thrown on the car. From Ballater to Birkhall, rain came down in sheets, but the crowds stayed until the car had passed.

Town, village and hamlet were full of cheering knots of people. At Birkhall, the housekeeper, Miss Mabel Gordon was waiting in the doorway to show them to the Royal suite. A new chapter in the Kent history had begun.

Finally, since heredity largely moulds mankind, let us consider the ancestral backgrounds of the Royal couple.

Prince Edward when he succeeded as second Duke of Kent on August 25th, 1942, was only six. He was the youngest Royal Duke since 1884, when Queen Victoria's grandson, Prince Charles Edward, was born Duke of Albany.

If a son and heir is born to the Royal couple he will bear the courtesy title of Earl of St. Andrews. If that happens, the Kent branch of the Royal family will be one of the few that have continued to the third generation in the male line.

The Dukedom of Kent had been bestowed once before in the Royal family. George III, who had seven grown-up sons, created three new Dukedoms, Kent, Sussex and Cambridge. His fourth son, Prince Edward, who became Duke of Kent in 1799 had, as his only child, Queen Victoria. Thus he was great-great-great-grandfather of the present Duke of Kent.

Though the Dukedom of Kent is comparatively new, there were three Earls of Kent, all of the House of Plantagenet, in the fourteenth century. Edmund of Woodstock, son of King Edward I and his second Queen, Margaret of France, was created Earl of Kent by his half-brother, Edward II. The notorious Queen Isabella ordered him to be beheaded at Winchester in 1330 for having tried to rescue his imprisoned unfortunate half-brother, the deposed king. The Earl of Kent's daughter, Joan, "the Fair Maid of Kent", was said to have been the owner of the dropped garter, which inspired Edward III to found the Order of the Garter. Her descendants, the Hollands and Greys, became in turn Earls of Kent. Henry Grey, Earl of Kent was raised to the Dukedom of Kent in 1710 by Queen Anne, but this became extinct on his death in 1740, sixty years before the Dukedom was bestowed on Queen Victoria's father.

On his mother's side the Duke of Kent has inherited the Royal blood of Greece, Denmark and Russia.

The ancestry of Princess Marina, Duchess of Kent, goes back to the famous Harold Bluetooth, tenth-century King of Denmark. His son, King Sweyn Forkbeard, conquered England in 1013, but died four months later. His son, Canute, later ruled both England and

Scandinavia. The Danish crown in time passed to Sweyn II, a son of Canute's sister, Astrid, and a first cousin of Harold of England who was slain at the Battle of Hastings. In 1448 the Danish crown passed to Christian I, first King of the House of Oldenburg, a direct ancestor in the male line of the Royal families of Greece and Denmark. Thus the Duke of Kent has Viking blood in his veins.

The Worsleys are one of those ancient families of squires who are part of the tapestry and background of England. They were land-owners in the North Riding of Yorkshire in the reign of Queen Elizabeth I. Their roots, however, go back much earlier to Lancashire. Their name derives from Worsley, now a suburb of Manchester where they were Lords of the Manor since Norman times.

The family is said to have been founded by Elias de Workesley who went with Duke Robert of Normandy on a crusade to the Holy Land. He was a man of enormous strength and valour and was known as Elias Gigas or Elias the Giant. It is recorded that "he fought many battles for the love of our Saviour Jesus Christ and obtained many victories. After many triumphs over the infidels he died at Rhodes, and was there buried".

Since few, except monks, could write in those days, there is, sad to say, no documentary evidence of his existence. The first Worsley of whom there is written proof is another Elias, born about eighty years after the Conquest.

The manor of Worsley went out of the family through the female line in the fourteenth century, and eventually was inherited by Francis Egerton, Duke of Bridgewater, "the Canal Duke" (1736–1803). He constructed a canal to Manchester in order to develop his coal mines at Worsley and later built the Bridgewater Canal to link Manchester with Liverpool.

Though their manor of Worsley was lost, the family continued to play an important part in Lancashire and beyond. William Worsley, who died in 1499, was Dean of St. Paul's and Canon of York. He was concerned in Perkin Warbeck's attempt to oust Henry VII from the throne and was convicted of high treason. However, through the efforts of his clergy he was pardoned and escaped the axe.

Charles Worsley of The Platt, Manchester, was the first Member for Manchester in Cromwell's Parliament, and one of the Protector's trusted generals. When Cromwell dismissed the Rump Parliament, he ordered Worsley to "take away these baubles".

The two most important branches of the Worsley family both left

Lancashire in Tudor times and established themselves at Appuldur-combe in the Isle of Wight, and at Hovingham in Yorkshire. Both received baronetcies. The Appuldurcombe branch was founded by James Worsley, Henry VIII's Keeper of the Wardrobe, who made him Captain (or Governor) of the Isle of Wight. This line, now extinct in the male line, is represented by the Earl of Yarborough, whose eldest son bears the courtesy title of Lord Worsley. Appuldurcombe, once a really splendid house near Ventnor, is now, alas, derelict. An obelisk to the Worsleys stands on the downs above the house.

The new Duchess of Kent's ancestor, Sir Robert Worsley of Booths, Lancashire, bought the manor of Hovingham in 1563. The house was rebuilt in the reign of George III by Thomas Worsley, M.P. for Calne, Wiltshire. He was Surveyor-General of the Board of Works, a con-noisseur and collector of books and pictures, and riding master to George III. The riding school which he built at Hovingham is a notice-able feature of the house. His grandson, Sir William Worsley, was given a baronetcy by Queen Victoria in 1838.

The new Duchess inherits not only Royal blood, but also that of the Lord Protector, Oliver Cromwell through the marriage of Thomas Worsley of Hovingham, to Mary, daughter of Sir Thomas Frankland, Bart. He was Postmaster-General in the reign of William and Mary.

Sir Thomas Frankland traced his descent to a Princess of the House of York, Anne, Duchess of Exeter, by her second marriage to Sir Thomas St. Leger. Anne, who is buried in St. George's Chapel, Wind-sor Castle, was a sister of Edward IV and Richard III. Elizabeth, Lady Frankland was a granddaughter of Oliver Cromwell.

The Duchess's father, Colonel Sir William Henry Arthington Worsley, fourth baronet, is Lord-Lieutenant of the North Riding of Yorkshire. Her mother is the daughter of the late Sir John Fowler Brunner, second baronet. The Brunners came from Bulach in the Canton of Zürich, Switzerland. Sir John's grandfather, the Rev. John Brunner, settled at Liverpool in 1832. The Brunners have a strain of Welsh blood, since the Duchess's grandmother, Lucy Marianne, Lady Brunner, was a daughter of Octavius Vaughan-Morgan, of a Brecon-shire family. His brother, Sir Walter Vaughan-Morgan, Bart., was Lord Mayor of London, 1905–6.

Finally there is a touch of Irish blood since the Duchess's great-grandfather, Arthington Worsley, married Marianne Heley-Hutchin-son, a niece of the third Earl of Donoughmore.

Thus begins a new chapter in the history of the Kent family—the family which has borne so much tragedy without complaint, and given an infinity of hard, devoted service.

Today, Princess Marina is, more than ever, a woman dedicated to the public weal. She epitomizes that too-often-forgotten principle of aristocracy, *noblesse oblige*. Her life is given to her family and to the State.

She has, now, not even a country house of her own. Her apartments in Kensington Palace are as busy with public affairs as a Chancellery. Her life is mapped and ordained to the service of Britain and her people. That is of her own choosing.

Her private hobbies remain, as always, cultivated, governed by her love of art, music and beauty.

Trained in the strict school of Royalty to Royal obligations, deeply religious, single-minded in devotion to her family, she mirrors Shakespeare's dictum on princes as:

> ". . . the glass, the school, the book,
>   Where subjects' eyes do learn, do read, do look."

Her memory and example will remain a sweet and lasting memorial of our present time.

Bibliography

My Fifty Years, by H.R.H. Prince Nicholas of Greece (1926).

Political Memoirs, by H.R.H. Prince Nicholas of Greece (1928).

Memoirs of H.R.H. Prince Christopher of Greece (1938).

H.R.H. The Duchess of Kent, by Baroness Helena Von-Der Hoven (1937).

Life Story of Princess Marina, by Grace Ellison (1934).

The Royal House of Greece, by Air Vice-Marshal Arthur S. Gould Lee (1948)

Rasputin and the Russian Court, by Charles Omessa (1918).

The Duchess of Kent, by Jennifer Ellis (1952).

Booklets of the Pitkin Press.

Index